D1507602

A LONG ROW
❧ TO HOE ❧

A LONG ROW TO HOE

BY
Billy C. Clark

INTRODUCTION BY
Gurney Norman

EDITED BY
James M. Gifford
Chuck D. Charles
Eleanor G. Kersey

BOOK DESIGN BY
Pamela K. Wise

THE JESSE STUART FOUNDATION

A Long Row to Hoe

Library of Congress Cataloging-in-Publication Data

Clark, Billy C., (Billy Curtis)
    A long row to hoe / Billy C. Clark.
    p. cm.
    Originally published: New York: Crowell, 1960.
    ISBN: 1-931672-04-0 : $15
    1. Clark, Billy C.—Biography—Youth. 2. Authors American—20th century—Biography. 3. Kentucky—social life and customs. 4. Catlettsburg (KY.)—Biography. I. Title.

Published by

Jesse Stuart Foundation
1645 Winchester Avenue
P.O. Box 669 • Ashland, KY 41105
(606) 326-1667 • JSFBOOKS.com

To my wife Ruth, my son Billy,
my daughter Melissa, and
my three grandchildren Benjamin,
Timothy, and Jodie Elisabeth.

ILLUSTRATIONS

Unless stated otherwise, all the photographic illustrations are from Arnold Hanner's private collection. The Jesse Stuart Foundation is very grateful for the assistance provided by the late Mr. Hanners, who was a highly regarded local historian and photographer.

Billy C. Clark

INTRODUCTION

I began reading Billy Clark's stories and books in the late 1950s on the recommendation of my writing teacher at the University of Kentucky, Dr. Hollis Summers. Billy had been Dr. Summers' student a few years before me, in the early and mid-1950s. Billy had not only written prolifically, he had also written professionally, publishing many stories in national magazines and even winning a book contract while he was still a student. By the time A Long Row to Hoe was published in 1960, when he was 32, Billy had four books in print, all published by major New York houses. Dr. Summers spoke often of his former student, pointing to Clark as an example of what was possible for a young writer with a natural language gift, many stories to tell, and fierce determination to get them told.

It excited me, as a student with my own interest in fiction writing, to know that Clark, who had so recently preceded me through the University, had found such early success. It was even more meaningful that the subjects of his stories were rural and small town Kentucky people, working people, often poor, many of whom still lived in "the old way", close to nature, working with their hands, at home in the woods and along the rivers from which they took much of their living in the form of wild game, fish, frogs, turtles, mink, and muskrat. The Eastern Kentucky coal-camp world I had grown up in was not identical with the river valleys Billy describes, but our boyhood worlds had much in common, and I identified deeply with what I found in his novels and short stories.

Of course I was familiar with other Kentucky writers such as Jesse Stuart, James Still, and Harriette Arnow, who also wrote about country people and whose stories and books were also published and well-reviewed in New York and Boston. Jesse Stuart stories in Esquire and Saturday Evening Post and James Still stories in The Atlantic Monthly and Virginia Quarterly Review and Billy Clark books from New York publishers had become events to anticipate rather than be surprised by.

All these writers were heroes and models for me, but I felt a special affinity for what Billy was doing, partly because we were more or less of the same generation but more importantly, for what Billy said and the way he said it. The clarity and directness of his style, his straightforward honesty of emotion, his sentiment without sentimentality, the artfully controlled vernacular language, his descriptions of nature that were at once realistic and lyrical, drew me in. It appealed to me that the world he described was a local one rendered in a style that adhered to methods and standards set by American writers such as Mark Twain, Sherwood Anderson, Ernest Hemingway, Katherine Ann Porter, John Steinbeck, whose books I was studying at the same time I began to read Clark's.

As a fiction writer, Billy has contributed honorably and memorably to the central tradition of the American short story and novel. What is so special about his autobiography, A Long Row to Hoe, is that it makes a radical departure from the traditional forms and gives us a book that is shocking in its originality.

The first and most obvious mark of originality in A

Long Row to Hoe is the fact that the author was so young when the book was published. How could a person only thirty two years old possibly have digested enough life experience to make serious readers want to know his life story?

After an opening scene which serves as the book's prologue, Clark begins his narrative-proper: "In nineteen years of growing up here in the valley, hunger was my most vivid memory; and an education was my greatest desire."

A page later, describing an experience of earliest boyhood: "We dug in the cold earth along the riverbanks for scrap iron from the old paddlewheel boats and barges, boats that had grounded in fogs and had been left to decay along the rivers. I dug in the earth for scrap iron to trade for cookies until my hands bled."

As a small boy prowling the streets of Catlettsburg and the banks of the nearby Big Sandy and Ohio Rivers, Clark witnessed: "When I could, I followed the fighters, keeping out of sight, and after they had fought I would search the earth all around to find money that might have dropped from their pockets. And so I followed Sid's dad and Little Pants now...Over the riverbanks they came, not walking but rolling. Little Pants was hollering. They fell hard under the trees and Little Pants grunted. I thought Sid's dad had surely crushed him. I sneaked closer to watch, then Sid's dad screamed as a knife blade went deep into his stomach. The knife went into the air again and again; red blood squirted on the low branches of the willows. And then the banks were quiet except for the light pat of Little Pants' feet over dried leaves and sand, and the splash he made as he slipped into the big Ohio."

For me, such scenes and such writing not only grab my attention, they hold it forever. A Long Row to Hoe is truly an unforgettable book. We label the book "an autobiography" and it is that, but it's more, something not so easy to define. The book creates its own category. It is alive, and a little mysterious, not just a world of experience Clark is describing but the way the experiences are connected, flowing one into the other on the river of Clark's language. The fabric of this writing contains a weave of true-life, never-heard-before stories, told by a writer who has given himself permission to say what he has to say, the way he wants to say it. The book presents endless stories, anecdotes, memories, scenes, adventures, jokes, speeches, information, lore, and character sketches not only of fascinating people but animals too, and even houses, and streets of the town and the nearby rivers and woods in which Clark always finds character. Clark writes in a voice that is honest, passionate, and compassionate, frequently humorous, sometimes pastoral, at other times angry at the human ignorance and cruelty and greed and social injustice he saw around him as a boy.

The class-awareness in A Long Row to Hoe is unconcealed. It is never a bitter awareness but it is unmistakably defiant. In A Long Row to Hoe, Clark is writing about poor people struggling at an elemental level to survive. He describes people without social or economic position or privilege, who get by on their skills, their wits, their cleverness, their ingenuity, their inherited knowledge of nature, and above all, their hardiness and determination.

Clark celebrates the dignity and worth and beauty of people that social snobs of the "higher" class would write off as "common." In the universe of <u>A Long Row to Hoe</u>, "common people" is a term of honor, a most American way of looking at things.

And yet, as truth-teller, Clark resists sentimentalizing his subjects. He presents pictures of human meanness and human beauty wherever he finds them. When people of any class are cruel to one other, or to animals, or just ignorant and selfish and destructive in their ways, he portrays it. Clark describes his beloved Big Sandy and Ohio Rivers as sources of life and infinite beauty, but he shows the rivers as forces of cruel, impersonal destruction as well. In his willingness to see nature and people at their best and worst, unflinchingly, Clark shows his loyalty to the community of which he is a native member by having a studied overview, by being the artist of it.

On the dustjacket of the original edition of <u>A Long Row to Hoe</u>, the publisher saw fit to append a subtitle: "Autobiography of a present-day Huckleberry Finn." While we appreciate the implicit compliment to Clark, and while there are obvious parallels between Clark and Twain, (for which reason <u>A Long Row to Hoe</u> is often used by teachers as a companion book to <u>Huckleberry Finn</u>), still, the author of the dustjacket blurb seems to have overlooked one of the major differences between Billy Clark and Huck Finn.

Huck Finn is a wonderful boy and a marvelous character, but he is essentially without family. The real heartbeat of <u>A Long Row to Hoe</u> is young Billy Clark's love for and loyalty to his family. He loves his father, a cobbler, skilled with his hands in many ways including his power to wring music from a fiddle; his mother, upholder of decency in the family, whose knuckles bleed from scrubbing clothes on a washboard; and the siblings, who possess a deep loyalty to one another. Both Huck and Clark (and many of Clark's fictional characters too) feel oppressed by and rebel against bourgeois pettiness, and both eventually "light out for the territory." But unlike Huck, the frontier Clark seeks education. As he explores that foreign field, he never forgets his family. In writing A Long Row to Hoe at the age of 32, Clark was announcing to himself and to the world that in social terms he, like Huck, was now free of the constraints of the rough world he grew up in. But in the realm of feelings, A Long Row to Hoe makes it clear that he is bound to that world forever.

The world Billy was born into in 1928 had changed utterly by 1960, when A Long Row to Hoe was published. The decades since 1960 have been a time of even more astounding change in the world around us and in our public and private lives. Who among us today is empowered to say just what the changes have been, what they signify and portend? No one fully comprehends our times, and there is great uncertainty and anxiety in our society because of it, as if all maps of a known way have been lost and all guiding knowledge forgotten. One reason there is so much anxiety in modern life is that most people only know how to do one thing, "one's job," one's specialty, so that even trained workers and professionals may abruptly find themselves obsolete. The model of the knowledgeable rural working person, male or female, one who is enterprising, versatile, multi-skilled in a range of arts and crafts and in possession of an inner certainty based on knowledge of the signs and markers of nature, has been lost. The people of the senior generation of Billy Clark's boyhood, and my own, who knew how to read the water, who understood the currents and depths, knew where the snags and shoals were and how to navigate safely past them even in flood time, are with us now mostly in the pages of books such as this one.

But the knowledge possessed by that older generation of rural Americans did not come from books. That generation had an understanding of life, a knowledge of the world, and a set of practical skills that is unimaginable to the generation born since 1960. They had a wisdom that lived in their minds and bodies and above all their memories, developed over time and handed down to them by people who had gone before. Memory does not seem to be highly valued or cultivated by our society now. It's as if it has become quaint, a vestige of old and somehow embarrassing days. The skills and virtues of the traditional country people, which in our time are being cast onto the junkheap of the consumer society at a frightening pace, were considered by them as plain and simple common sense. It is common sense when people remember to take care of what sustains them, whether it be tools, customs, land and water or books and education. In the context of caring for that which sustains, A Long Row to Hoe is more than a nice-to-have book, it is a necessary one.

"An education was my greatest desire" Billy tells us early in his testimony. That desire led him to become a writer and a teacher. Perhaps in a future installment of his autobiography, Mr. Clark will speak of his long career as a college teacher and give us the benefit of that part of his experience, for I know that side of his working life has been an inspiration to many people.

This edition of A Long Row to Hoe is the first in a series of reprints of books by Billy Clark, an ambitious project sponsored by the Jesse Stuart Foundation that will eventually see all of Clark's books in print again. The Foundation has already succeeded in returning many of Jesse Stuart's major works to print, and it has a wide range of other regional publications in various developmental stages. It is important work the Foundation is doing, work rooted in living American culture and dedicated to readers of the future. Like many hundreds of thousands of other people, I appreciate the Foundation's long-range vision and commitment and the cultural common sense that underlies it. It is refreshing to see such important work being done, not for political or financial gain, but because it is a good and healthy thing to do.

Gurney Norman

CHAPTER 1

❦

"So you're actually planning to go away to college?"

John Simpler walked toward where I stood overlooking the Big Sandy and Ohio rivers. He focused his eyes on me only momentarily, and then glanced beyond quickly, as if he expected the two streams to be lapping over the rim of the town. Both had risen slowly during the night, creeping up the banks, and the swirl of their muddy water hummed like an autumn wind.

John Simpler was a thin man, and the most noticeable thing about him was his pale face. Years had stretched the skin tight, and wherever it crossed the bones of his face, tiny red veins showed. To me he symbolized the clique that controlled the town and most of the people in the valley. He was a merchant of Catlettsburg who owned a two-story brick store standing close enough to the two rivers for their shouldering to be heard from the front of the building. John Simpler feared the hum of these rivers.

I had come to the river early today, so early that wisps of morning fog remained. My plans were to take one last look at it before leaving town. Time had narrowed down and now one hundred thirty miles separated me from the beginning of the greatest dream I had ever had: entering the University of Kentucky at Lexington. I had hoped to leave town without having to hear more questions. Why did they ask about my plans to attend the university? They knew all the answers. They had calculated my beginning and end since the day I was born. They could have told you how I

View of Kentucky, Ohio, and West Virginia, from Catlettsburg.

"I stood over-looking the Big Sandy and Ohio Rivers."

would, or should, end up according to their little map. Did something go wrong? Or was this merely the dying plunge, that my kind of people made in their efforts to break from the pattern? That was it. Once the plunge had been made, I would crouch back to my rightful place as others had done, quivering like a whipped dog. And they would say, I told you so.

John Simpler's coming here so early of the morning was not to wish me luck on what lay ahead. He had come to look once again at the two rivers, now that they were so close to his store. His clique could not control the rivers as they controlled people. About the rivers, they could only guess. But John Simpler could be sure of one thing: if the water came over the banks, he must move his merchandise from the first floor of his building to the second; if it came higher, he must move everything he owned across town to high ground. He had never been close enough to the rivers to know their signs and their moods, and sometimes he had moved without having to move at all. But in misjudging the rivers he was not alone. With him had been practically the whole population of Catlettsburg.

And now John Simpler humped his back, resembling a bullfrog ready to jump from the hand that is about to snatch him, and peered over the bank at the rivers.

"Even if you don't make it to school," he said, "you're lucky to get out of town. The water looks like it'll come all the way this time."

The Big Sandy still seemed shallow to me. In the center of the small river a great white sand bar nosed out of the surface—but not so much now that the rivers were moody.

The Morse Opera House during the 1913 flood.

"But John Simpler could be sure of one thing; if the water came over the banks, he must move his merchandise from the first floor of his building to the second; if it came higher, he must move everything he could across town to high ground."

Usually the sand bar stuck far enough above the surface for the wind to push waves over it, and to me there had never been anything prettier. The current of the Big Sandy was eating away at the top of the sand bar. A current meant a moving river. Now the current was an indication that the bigger Ohio could take away the excess water from the small river, caused by heavy rains farther up. But even the great Ohio could not absorb so much water in one gulp. It would suck at it slowly, pulling its insides from underneath and then, and only then, would the bloated Big Sandy fall from the rim of the town.

But John Simpler did not see the current. He thought only of running from these rivers. And he saw that they had both climbed steadily up the banks during the night.

"I don't believe they'll come over the banks," I said.

John Simpler looked quickly at me. He scratched his face and where he scratched the color changed.

"What makes you think they won't?" he asked.

"There's too much current in the big river," I said. "If the current remains they should fall some before dark."

I watched him eye the current again, as if wondering whether or not he should change his own opinion. His kind had been running from these rivers long before I was born in the valley. They feared the water worse than a copperhead snake, since many of their businesses depended on what the water did. But after all their years of squinting their eyes over the banks they knew little about the muddy currents.

As close as I had lived with these two rivers, I could never be sure of what they would do. But I had learned to judge them pretty well. In this country the sky could be as blue as an egg of a robin one minute and black as the wings of a crow the next. Rain could come before you could find shelter, swelling the feeder streams along the course of the Big Sandy until the river rose over the town.

"Well," John Simpler said, "it could be you know what you're talking about. I guess you've been along these rivers more than most people here. I used to see you going out every day in a joeboat."

In this he was right. Many times of the early spring and

summer I had gone to raise my trotline at the mouth and to check turtle nibs tied to the willows along the banks, then oared on up the Big Sandy to raise a second trotline. In winter I traveled the rivers to look about my steel traps stretched along the shores to take mink and muskrat. Often of the mornings fog would drift heavy over the surfaces of the rivers and I could hardly see the bank. I had learned something of the fog on these rivers. If you bear it out, as the morning grows old a wind will come to thin it. And the wind plays in the trees along the banks so that even inside the fog patches it can be heard and it will tell you the location of the bank and chart your course.

Late of the evenings when the wind was low in the trees and the rivers were calm and the catbird, thrush, killdeer, and sandpipers hunted the trees for cover at night, I had drifted down river after baiting the lines, hoping to catch me a frog or two before I tied in. I had seen John Simpler then, coming to take a last look at the rivers before going across town to his home. I can't remember him or the others that gathered along the rivers ever waving or even making a gesture at me. Then it would have meant something.

There had been times too when I had peddled turtles, catfish, and frogs on the streets of Catlettsburg that John Simpler, squinting up and down the street to be sure that he would not be seen buying from me, had motioned me to his store. Not to the front, but down the small alley to the side door. He had been a particular man. He would buy no frog, turtle, or catfish unless it was cleaned. And you could not clean them along the riverbanks; he wouldn't trust that they

Division Street, Catlettsburg

"There had been times too when I had peddled turtles, catfish, and frogs on the streets of Catlettsburg..."

were fresh taken. Neither would he pay extra for the cleaning. A man would have demanded more; a boy as hungry as I must clean for free.

"How long these frogs been out of the river, boy?" he'd say.

"Fetched them last night," I would answer. And using the alley to the back room of his store I would clean them— a bull nickel for a small frog and ten cents for a large one. Either was a small price for a frog. Catching one required time and hard work.

However, time had changed many things. Now for the first time in my life I felt independent. No more long nights along the rivers searching for bullfrogs; no more backbreaking work of scuddling a joeboat with one arm while I baited a trotline by sliding it over my legs, dodging the hooks and at the same time trying to skin on a minnow or crawdad or worm as each hook passed. Only memories and the rivers remained.

"I've been with the river a lot," I said, thinking of what John Simpler had said.

John Simpler looked at me and said, "You know, your trying to go to college puzzles me. Most people generally stick to their raising. Your dad has always been a fiddle player and a shoe cobbler. Your mother came from up the Big Sandy. I never knew either of them were educated people."

"They aren't," I answered.

"Well, I can tell you this much—" he said, "you're a fool if you once get out of the town and then come back. That is, if you figure on doing something with your education."

"Why?" I asked.

"You'll be judged by what your people have always been here in the valley and what they are now."

"That's all right with me," I said.

"Take my advice," he said. "I hear they're hiring some at the steel mill below Ashland. If you can get on, you better take it. If you don't you'll be back home in a week, broke."

John Simpler took a quick glance at the rivers and walked away. I had been given the same advice by others. Funny, but these words would not stick. The ones that stuck were words that I had heard long ago, from my father. I was seven years old, and we had just lost almost all we owned to the floods. Dad carried me to safety on his back. He said "Poor folks have a long row to hoe in this world."

ii

In nineteen years of growing up here in the valley, hunger was my most vivid memory; and an education was my greatest desire. Recently the questions and doubts of the clique had added another feeder stream—a new desire. I wanted to prove them wrong and upset the pattern. They couldn't ration out desire and determination as they had the laws of the town. Instead, both were given freely to the poor as well as the prosperous by a Great Man whose hands could move a cloud aside and allow the sun to come through in the dead of winter, melting patches of snow to allow a common sparrow to find food.

Then I thought to myself: Just as you have mapped my destiny, John Simpler, so I have mapped yours. I'll see the day that your bones will be so brittle you won't be able to walk to look over the rivers. You'll curse both age and the rivers, just as you've gone through life cursing everything else. And the sparrows will circle and build nests in the loose bricks of your building and the rivers will continue to rise. For me the fog has lifted. But all the winds that have blown in the valley can't thin the fog that comes to the eyes of an old man. And the rivers will defeat you in the end, making your building a little more than useless, just as it has destroyed most of the other old buildings in Catlettsburg.

Chow Burton was a member of your clique. He used to sit in front of his store just like you—a big man, better than six feet tall and well over two hundred pounds, who had more breeds in him than a mountain cur dog. His eyes were slanted, and so he was said to be a Chinaman. He operated a junk shop in one side of his building and a cookie bakery in the other. When winter came to the valley, he didn't wear heavy socks like most of the people. He wrapped his feet and legs in old newspapers—because he was so stingy, people said. I remember the smell of his gingersnap cookies drifting over the street, a sweet smell that drew boys to the front of the store thick as wild bees are drawn to the bloom of the poplar tree. The smell of those gingersnap cookies made us kids do strange things. We dug in the cold earth along the riverbanks for scrap iron from the old paddlewheel boats and barges, boats that had grounded in fogs and had been left to decay along the rivers. I dug in the earth for scrap iron to trade for cookies until my hands were raw. I swam the width of the Big Sandy to the West Virginia point, in water cold enough to freeze the feathers on a duck's back, to dig where an old showboat had run aground many years ago. And after all the swimming in the cold water and digging in the mud and sand, the iron was weighed on scales that made them weigh only as much as Chow Burton wanted.

Chow Burton did not like for us to gather around his store to stare at the cookies. He called us river trash. He would let his cookies mold before he would give us any, or feed them to stray dog while we stood by and watched. But

Chow Burton had made us experts at lying and cheating, too. Iron pipes were filled with sand and the ends battered together to make them weigh more. The pounds that Chow Burton marked down were the ones added by the sand. And when his eyes became weaker, tin cans were battered inside old aluminum pots and both sold to him for aluminum. Copper-coated wire was sold for solid copper. And even now while Chow Burton was weighing our scrap we stole from his own stock and resold it to him.

We remembered the many times he had watched us stand in front of the store, hungry for the cookies. And when his leg grew too old to catch us, we would run in front of the store chanting:

> "Chinaman, Chinaman eats dead rats,
> Chews them up like gingersnaps."

"You, boy!" Chow Burton would say, singling one of us out.

"Come here. You watch my cookies for me so the other boys don't steal 'em and I'll give you all you can eat."

But, like drift from the river gathering in one pile, we stuck together. Whoever had been singled out would pass the cookies behind his back to the rest of us until the stand was empty. And Chow Burton would curse us with a voice that carried as far as the smell of his gingersnap cookies.

Front Street, Catlettsburg.

"Sid's dad was killed on Bloody Front the same summer that Sid spilled the crawdads."

CHAPTER 2

Sid Taylor and I were in the fourth grade at school. We had a lot in common. Sid Taylor's hair was as long as mine and his clothes had as many patches. His hair was a flaming red and freckles covered his skin. When he laughed Sid was one of the funniest sights I have ever seen. Near his right eye there was a large brown freckle as big as a bird egg, and if he laughed or moved his face the large freckle changed to many shapes. I used to watch him at the edge of a marble ring when he stooped to shoot his taw. He would draw up his face before he shot, and the brown freckle near his eye would stretch out and wiggle like a red fishing worm out in the hot sun. If he missed, he would stretch his face long, making a night crawler of the freckle.

Considering the fact that Sid's hair was red (I thought red hair belonged on a girl along with freckles) he was a pretty smart boy. If I'd had the red hair and the freckles, I'd have been ashamed of both. Sid Taylor wasn't. In fact, he was quick to take advantage of the big freckle near his eye. He knew that most everyone at school stared at it. He knew they watched each time he moved his face to see what the freckle would do. They tried to guess ahead of the freckle. Many were willing to bet marbles that they were right as to the shape it would take. And Sid took all betters. And he took all marbles, since he could control the shape of the freckle.

Early that spring I crossed the town toward the rivers, carrying a can of soft crawdads that I hoped to sell to some fisherman. In the spring the white perch ran, and any fisherman knew that they would almost walk out on the bank for a soft crawdad. I had ten soft crawdads in the can; it had taken a full day's work at Catletts Creek to gather them. Actually, there were fourteen crawdads in my can, but only ten were soft ones. Four of them were—or I should say had been—hard-shelled crawdads a short while before. I had helped them along in becoming soft. I needed fourteen. At two for a penny I would have seven cents, enough for a loaf of bread. I was hungry. I figured by the time the fisherman who bought them found out, I would either be gone or would have enough head start to outrun him along the banks of the rivers.

When the sun comes warm enough to pop leaves on the limbs of the trees and sifts through them to take the bite from the winter water, the crawdads back slowly from under rocks and old logs along the bottom of the creek. Now their shells are as black as the hull of a walnut that has spent the winter in the hills. They creep toward the edges of the banks where the water is shallow and warmed by the sun, their long black feelers moving with the current and shooting up like antennas trying to grab hold of the rays of the sun. And here they wait for nature to peel the rock-hard shells from them, like shucking ears of corn, giving them a new shell that will remain soft for a few days. So soft is the new shell that if the crawdad is held between two fingers it will droop over like wet string.

This day nature did not seem in the least concerned with the fact that the white perch were running or that I could sell the crawdads like hotcakes. And after taking only ten soft crawdads I decided to help nature out a little. The trouble was, I could shuck away the hard shell of the crawdad but I could not give it the soft, new skin that nature gave. What was left was only the white flesh that resembled soft skin. The truth would not be known until the fisherman put the crawdad on a hook. Then, without the summer skin to hold the flesh together, the crawdad would fall apart.

Where the town dips over to meet the rivers, I stopped to make sure that the four peeled crawdads were at the bottom of the can, under the others. Just then I saw Sid Taylor, carrying a tin can in his hand. I frowned. There might not be many fishermen out today. Perhaps the crawdads would be hard to sell. I was sure that Sid had a can of crawdads, too. What I couldn't be sure of was how many, and whether they were soft or hard.

Luck seemed to be with me. As I watched Sid he turned sideways and began to back toward the rivers, keeping his eyes on the door of the saloon here on the corner of the street. Sid was watching for his dad, and there was every chance in this world that if he watched long enough he would see him come staggering out. Sid's dad spent about as much time in the saloon as the bartender.

As Sid backed up, he tripped, and into the air he went, can and all. I watched the crawdads hit the hot bricks, going quickly in all directions. Most of them were hard-shelled; soft ones would have spattered on the hot bricks and been fried. The big black crawdads got their bearings now and backed toward the rivers. "Oh, golly damn!" Sid hollered at the top of his voice.

About this time two women walked out of John

Simpler's store. They stopped and stared at Sid. Sid's long hair drooped below his shoulders and then over his face and eyes as he bent to scoop up the crawdads.

"You black sons of bitches!" he yelled, grabbing for the crawdads and falling again.

One of the women said, "Listen to the language of that little heathen! My boy Jim's in the same room with him at school. Look at that hair! No wonder there's an epidemic of lice at the schoolhouse each year."

I was too close to the women for comfort myself. I hunkered at the corner of the saloon, peeking around the corner. The wind, on its way to the rivers caught me full in the face, lifted my hair into the air like a bunch of crabgrass ready to be snipped with the cutters, and then let it droop to my shoulders. "Damn you to hell and old Miss Stigill!" Sid yelled, flat on his belly now, and he reached out and squashed one of the big crawdads with the palm of his hand. He lifted his head and stared straight into the eyes of the women. With his feet moving like a buzz saw he was on his feet and over the riverbank.

"I'll tell you there ought to be something done about this river trash!"

The women had it all wrong. Sid wasn't river trash. He didn't live along the rivers at all. And I thought that Sid was really lucky where he lived—in a log cabin deep in a hollow back of town. At nights he climbed a ladder made of sassafras sprouts to bed down in the attic of the cabin. There were eight in Sid's family and they all slept in the same bed just as we did at our house. The birds roosted in the attic with Sid and he got to lie there and listen to them quarrel all night. Sometimes when Sid's dad got tired of staying over on Bloody Front, he would walk up the hollow to the cabin. You could hear him for a long distance, "Come out, Lilly Bell! Come sit with me in the lovers' moonlight!"

Lilly Bell was Sid's mother, and she did not come out. She quickly gathered her family in the attic, taking a bucket of scalding water with her and pulling the ladder up behind them. Sid's dad would stand under the hole where they had disappeared and say, "Come down, Lilly Bell. Come down from the high heavens like a bird and chirp to me. You know I love you."

Timber run at the mouth of the Big Sandy River, Catlettsburg.

"They'd ride the logs to the mouth of the Big Sandy, spend their earnings in the saloons, and then walk all the way back on foot."

But what came down was the bucket of hot water. Sid's dad would go sprawling on the floor, moaning as if he were dying and at the same time keeping one eye peeled toward the attic to see if Lilly Bell felt sorry for him and was coming down. She wouldn't and he'd become so mad that he'd shake the rafters in the house before he left again for Bloody Front. He was said to be sleeping with a black woman named Hattie Sims who ran a bootleg joint on Bloody Front, catering to the whites. If Hattie ever threw anything at him, you can bet your bottom dollar it was whiskey. I used to carry sandwiches to the drunks there and her place was full of the stuff.

The woman that had scared Sid over the riverbanks, before she'd heard a tenth of the language Sid knew, was Effie Larks. She was important in the town! Her boy Jim was in our grade at school. I envied Jim Larks. His hair was forever being cut by a barber in town and his clothes looked like they had just been taken from the store window. He walked around bragging about his grandpa owning a fleet of paddle wheels and sidewheelers back when the town lived from the rivers.

Dad said, "You know, Billy, these rivers have done strange things to the people of this town. Even though the Big Sandy is dead many still live by the ghost. They keep the reputations they claim some kin built along the rivers long ago. This makes them important without them having to do anything theirselves. But the paddle wheels didn't build this town; it was the men who rode the logs that did it. They'd ride the logs to the mouth of the Big Sandy, spend their earnings in the saloons, and then walk all the way back on foot."

After that Jim Larks didn't seem so important to me.

ii

Sid's dad was killed on Bloody Front the same summer that Sid spilled the crawdads. I was there when he came rolling out of the saloon door with a bear hug on a small black man called Little Pants. Little Pants janitored around the saloons. During the days, he walked around the tables gathering beer and whiskey from glasses that whites hadn't taken the last gulp from. When he'd gathered enough to fill a glass, he'd go off in a corner and drink it.

I thought this ruckus now was just another fight. Fights happened often here. The men burst out of the swinging doors on their way to the riverbanks to settle their quarrels. When I could, I followed the fighters, keeping out of sight, and after they had fought I would search the earth all around to find money that might have dropped from their pockets. And so I followed Sid's dad and Little Pants now.

Over the river bank they came, not walking but rolling. Little Pants was hollering. They fell hard under the trees and Little Pants grunted. I thought Sid's dad had surely crushed him. I sneaked closer to watch, then Sid's dad screamed as a knife blade went deep into his stomach. The knife went into the air again and again; red blood squirted on the low branches of the willows. And then the banks were quiet except for the light pat of Little Pants' feet over dried leaves and sand, and the splash he made as he slipped into the big Ohio.

People from the saloon carried Sid's dad up the bank and stretched him on a long wooden bench outside the saloon door. "Lord!" a woman screamed, "the least someone can do is cover him up!" They brought one of the white cloths from a table inside the saloon and placed it over him, and the white sheet soaked blood like sand soaks water.

"Get that black man!" someone yelled and several men ran into the willows. But they didn't catch Little Pants. Not along these rivers. He knew them too well. In the summer and winter he slept there. And now he weaved through the trees like an eel trying to get back to water and swam the big Ohio to the far side. Here he stayed along the banks for several weeks living off corn and roots and raw fish that he caught. And then one day, of his own free will, he crossed the big river again and gave himself up on the Kentucky shore and was sent to the pen.

"Steal a chicken and they hang you—" people said, "kill a man and you get two years' free living on taxpayers' money!"

Many claimed that Sid's dad had it all coming to him. The only shame was to be killed by a black man. He had been bullying Little Pants around on Bloody Front for many years, because he figured Little Pants couldn't defend himself. But others said that Little Pants had planned the whole thing. He hadn't liked the idea of Sid's dad sleeping with Hattie Sims and getting whiskey for doing it.

At night now, and for many nights to come, I closed my eyes and saw the long blade of the knife sink into white flesh. And in my dreams the very sheet on which I slept turned red like the saloon tablecloth, that had been washed in the rivers and placed back over a table inside the swinging doors.

"Old Paddle Creek Bourbon Whisky"
Made in Catlettsburg, Kentucky.

Log run on the Big Sandy River, Catlettsburg.

"...and yet he could step on a raft of logs and ride them as light as a sparrow."

CHAPTER 3

About this time I had a notion that one of my grandpas might have been a river-boat captain owning a great fleet. First it was only a day-dream. I had learned that a dream can make living easy, if only for a little while.

After a few days the dream got out of hand. Not only had I become dead sure that my dream had legs, but if anyone at the schoolhouse even so much as mentioned that perhaps only one of my grandpas had owned a paddle wheel I would have fist fought them. Trouble was, I was the only one at school that could see my dream. Not one of them acted any different toward me than they always had. How often I hung around the schoolhouse yard wishing that there was some way for my dream to walk out of my head to be seen and read like pages of a book. Finally I knew that I could carry the dream no longer.

"Dad," I said, in the basement where he was fixing an old pair of shoes, "was Grandpa Clark or Grandpa Hewlett a river-boat captain?"

Dad stuck a dozen tacks in his mouth and straightened the shoe on the last. While he hesitated, I looked around to make sure that none of my brothers or sisters could over-hear me. They had laughed at too many of my dreams. A frown came to Dad's face and he spit one of the tacks out between his lips. And in the period of time it took him to spit out the tack, his frown had shrunk my dream until I would have settled right then and there for only one paddle wheel owner in the family.

"Your Grandpa Clark was seldom near the rivers." He hammered at the shoe and spit out another tack. "But your Grandpa Hewlett was a riverman. Lived his whole life on the rivers. Big man. Weighed well over two hundred pounds and yet could step on a raft of logs and ride them as light as a sparrow. Had music in him to give him balance." Dad leaned on the last. "They had to build a special coffin for him. He never owned or piloted a boat, but he was the best sawyer and rafter and rider that ever was in the valley. Come down the river with his fiddle in one hand and a steering oar in the other."

My dream had been punctured. But before all hope could leak out I began to think, Dad should know about his own father, but maybe he didn't know all about Grandpa Hewlett. Mom would.

"No," Mom said. "Your Grandpa Hewlett was a sawyer. Cut timber and rode it down the Big Sandy until the day he died." Another dream was gone. Grandpa Hewlett had been a timberman, never a boat pilot. But he had been part of the Big Sandy and, according to Dad, the part that had really built the town. Now in the quiet hours of the days Mom spoke of him and I listened.

Grandpa Hewlett had been a man of tremendous strength—broad as the handle of a double-bitted ax, and a great flock of auburn hair as thick on his chest as on his head. On the coldest days of winter he walked among the trees with his shirt unbuttoned, letting the winter air in to dry the sweat. Setting his feet solid in the earth, he would lift a black gum log that usually required two men to carry it to the saw.

Many years ago log rafts had been pegged together as

Timber scene on the Big Sandy River, Catlettsburg.

"Many years ago log rafts had been pegged together as far up as the breaks of the Big Sandy."

far up as the breaks of the Big Sandy. Grandpa Hewlett had rode them out of the currents, bringing them to Catlettsburg. But in his time the slopes were slaughtered of trees, and the deserted hills sprouted third- and fourth-growth timber. As the timber disappeared, so did the importance of the town. At one time there had been twenty-six saloons on Bloody Front and never foot room along the brass rails of the bars. Today, the streets were vacant except for the three saloons when the town was "wet" and three bootleg joints when the town was "dry."

But cutting timber had been too deep in Grandpa Hewlett's blood to stop when the trees were gone from the valley. And one day, taking a change of clothes, he journeyed down the Ohio and then on foot as far as North Carolina. "Carliny," Mom called it—"all the way to Carliny," she said, squinting her mouth to one side and looking proud.

North Carolina! I thought. How far away was it? Probably halfway around the world and back. If a journey like that wouldn't beat just being a plain river-boat owner and pilot, I thought, I'd bite into a creek shiner. Now, what would they think when I told them at school!

Nothing. No one seemed to be impressed by the journey. The big map at the schoolhouse made the distance he had traveled look but inches away. When I spoke of this giant, his great flock of auburn hair blowing in the winter winds, his shirt unbuttoned, lifting the huge logs over his shoulder and pinning them to others to make a raft big enough to hold him, it widened no eyes but mine.

I came to see that I'd have to settle for what my people had been in the valley, not what I wanted them to be.

ii

Even though Grandpa Hewlett had been as rugged as the hills around him, he had a heart as soft as the morning glories that climb the brown stalks of corn here in the valley during the autumn. He was a fiddle player; music was in his body, and his body was big enough to hold all the music of the hills.

Many years ago he had shuffled over the knoll from his house, deep in a hollow twelve miles up the Sandy, and had traveled to the lowlands along the Big Sandy. He walked into a patch of corn, searched the field closely with his eyes and chose the biggest stalk of corn he could find. It was in the fall and the corn had been tanned by an autumn wind and seasoned by the sun. And here along the banks of the river he sat to cut the great stalk of corn at two joints, hollowing the pulp out of the stalk and then plugging both ends. He cut one half of the stalk away, slitting it from end to end, leaving four slender natural fibers of the corn to match the four strings of a fiddle. He took the cornstalk fiddle back home and for his bow he pulled the hairs from the tail of a big white-slatted work mule that belonged to my great-grandpa Jephthah Bonaparte Hewlett and stretched them over a hickory sprout. To cut away some of the roughness of the hairs crossing the strings he rosined the bow with sap from a white pine tree.

While he worked the long bottoms along the Big Sandy, his fiddle rested at the end of the rows somewhere in the sand where the sun would not warp it. Along the hillsides he hung it to a low branch of a tree while he planted. And when he got his first job cutting timber, he took the fiddle into the timber camps.

Yet the music that came from the cornstalk fiddle was not clear. There was a screech that did not belong in the softness of a mountain ballad. So he set his heart to owning a real wooden fiddle. And he bargained one day with a boat captain to bring him one from down the Ohio.

The day came when the fiddle was in his hands—a real honest-to-goodness wooden fiddle, and one of the first real fiddles in the Big Sandy Valley. Grandpa Hewlett turned from the mouth of the Big Sandy, and following the path along its course back to the hills, he fiddled almost every step of the way, spreading the music over the valley like a summer wind.

And when the time come for him to go courting he took the fiddle with him. "Till the day he left the valley," Dad said, "Jim Hewlett claimed that it was the sweet music of the fiddle that won Emmazett Stuart's heart."

"I don't know why Mason lies so," Mom would say. "Your grandma was a righteous woman."

But the fiddle was said to have coaxed Grandma Emmazett into marrying him. It also was said that soon after Grandma Emmazett got converted and baptized in the water of the Big Sandy, the fiddle became an instrument of the devil. No worse sin could befall a person than to draw the bow over the strings of a fiddle. The music could travel as quickly here in the hills as the fleety feet of Satan. And the sins of a fiddle player were equal only to those of the square dancer. One made the other.

Grandpa Hewlett was dead set on keeping Grandma Emmazett's heart with the music of his fiddle, tantalizing her with pulls of the bow. Grandma Emmazett was dead set on breaking him of the fiddle and pulling back the clouds so that he could "see the light of salvation."

She nagged and nagged each time he brought the fiddle back from the timber camps. And the nagging became so great that one day he placed the fiddle aside. She coaxed him on. The day would come when he would have to leave this earthly valley. Was he prepared to go? Could he say that he had walked the straight and narrow path?

A change came over Grandpa Hewlett. Instead of moving about as free as a mountain wind he began to sit by himself, staring into space as if the weight of the biggest black oak in the valley was on his shoulders. Thinking the time had come for him to receive the Spirit, Grandma Emmazett made arrangements for the circuit rider to stop on his next trip up the valley.

Fire and damnation came from the lips of the circuit rider, bringing tears to Grandpa Hewlett's eyes, and to the joy of Grandma Emmazett he agreed to walk forth to the water of the Big Sandy and be washed of his sins.

A large crowd of men and women from the hills gathered along the banks of the river. The women came to show their joy and bring well wishes to Grandma Emmazett. The men gathered to see if their eyes were really looking at Grandpa Hewlett, and then they began to place bets that the small circuit rider wouldn't be able to dip the great trunk of Grandpa Hewlett into the river and bring him up again. Three to one that Grandpa Hewlett would have to swim his way to the surface.

But the small, beady-eyed circuit rider proved to be an experienced man. He led Grandpa Hewlett into the river, and standing on a large rock so that he could reach Grandpa's shoulders he dipped him into the river and brought up the weight as easy as lifting a dry log to the surface.

"How do you feel, Jim Hewlett?" The circuit rider

asked as he watched the huge man shake the water from his great flock of auburn hair.

"Easy as fallin' off a saw log backwards," Grandpa Hewlett said. "Don't feel a damn bit different though."

But still the music of the fiddle would not leave Grandpa Hewlett. He grieved for it so much that one day he walked to the small outhouse where he had hung up his fiddle and he lifted it from the battered case. He had lost faith. He had backslid. And with tears streaming down his face he pulled the bow over the strings and he was happy again.

"You must repent!" Grandma Emmazett said to him. And she did manage to coax him to the small log church near the mouth of the Big Sandy. And here he sat along the wooden benches, grumbling. There were times, Dad said, that he could be heard whistling low a fiddle tune right inside the church. Eventually, Grandma Emmazett refused to listen to the music at all. She declared that the fiddle could not be brought inside the house.

Before long Grandpa Hewlett couldn't be coaxed. He decided the greatest gift that a man could possess was to play the fiddle. And he walked the hills playing the fiddle faster than the winds could blow.

Being a timber man, he could take an ax in one hand and his fiddle in the other, and find company where he would be respected. Following the timber, he was now away from home much of the time. And at nights while Grandma Emmazett sat inside the log church far down the currents of the Big Sandy, he would squat somewhere up river under the shadows of the trees and play his fiddle. Under the trees a huge fire would be spreading shadows every which way and the feet of the square dancers would be flying high into the air like dry leaves in a wind storm.

He often stopped to visit Mom and Dad, who had not long been married. "You ought to play the fiddle, Mason," Grandpa Hewlett would say, and he'd sit in the split-bottomed chair and bear to his bow, free to play here as long as he had mind to. "Got no one to take up playing once I'm gone. All girls in my family. Not a chance for a fiddle player."

And Grandpa Hewlett would set his mind to the fiddle, and he'd play and sing:

"They grew and grew in the old church yard,
They could not grow no higher,
And there they tied in a true love knot
The red rose and the briar."

"Look at them long, lean fingers of yours, Mason," Grandpa would say again. "Useless as a sumac sprout. Fiddlin' fingers." And then he'd set his chin on the fiddle again and grin as he watched Dad pat his foot to keep time.

In the latter years before he died, Grandpa Hewlett left his fiddle at Dad's when he stopped. "To agg me on," Dad said. Grandpa Hewlett was afraid to face up to Grandma Emmazett, Mom would say, "All men have a sneakin' streak to 'em."

So Dad picked the fiddle up and slid his fingers over the slender neck. After Grandpa Hewlett died, he was buried here in the hills, overlooking the valley and the Big Sandy. And just as surely as if the strength, tenderness, and love for the fiddle had seeped from Grandpa Hewlett's fingers into Dad's, Dad played the fiddle like the wind.

iii

Uncle Dave Hewlett was one of the last of his generation to leave the valley. He lived with his brother Frank twelve miles up the Big Sandy and six miles deep in a hollow. You reached his home by traveling the bed of a creek during dry spells or along a crude path high on the banks whenever the creek was flowing.

We did not make many trips during the year to Uncle Dave's. But as sure as daylight will break again over these hills, one of the trips would be just before Decoration Day. On this day we would gather daisies, roses, and many other wild flowers to sprinkle over the graves of our dead, and we cleaned the cemeteries and built up the mounds where the snows of winter had sunk them.

We all gathered in long lines and marched up the hills to pick flowers. The men carried tubs or half-hogshead barrels and the older boys carried buckets of water. Girls carried lunch baskets and balls of string to tie the flowers. The women carried knives, to cut them. They also carried children too small yet to walk.

Along the slopes grew the wild daisies and over the big gray rocks trailed the mountain rose. Here we set our tubs down and emptied the buckets of water into them. We gathered the flowers and tied them in bunches and placed them in the tubs of water so they would not wilt.

With so many people gathering them here around home, the flowers were becoming scarce. But there were still plenty at Uncle Dave's. So deep in the hollow, no one would touch the flowers except us.

His small gray-slabbed house stood in a deep hollow. The grass was always tall in the yard and, beside the house, rock cliffs slid into the earth with caves under them, and opossum grape vines hung over the caves like brown eyebrows over deep, dark eyes.

Uncle Dave was blind, yet long before we reached the yard he would be standing at the edge of the porch waving his arms. His ears were as keen as a squirrel's.

"Now you stay with your Uncle Dave, Billy," Mom would say.

And Uncle Dave would turn his blind eyes toward the sound of Mom's voice, grin, and say to her, "Lord, Berthy, don't you worry about old Dave. You come here to pick flowers for the dead and on this day you think old Dave needs tending to. What about all the other days of the year I'm here by myself? You go on to the hills and leave Billy here with me. Not to tend me but just to keep me company for a spell." And then he would sweep his hand in the direction of the yard. "You mind and don't pick the heads from the flowers here in the yard. I love to smell 'em. I can tell the seasons by smell. Bet the flowers are pretty now that they're in bloom, ain't they, Berthy?"

This was the one time that I loved to be left behind. I would rather have sat there with Uncle Dave than to go chasing lizards over the rocks with my three brothers, fooling Mom into thinking we were all looking for flowers.

I loved to sit on the porch and watch Uncle Dave's long white beard blow in the winds that turned the edges of the rocks and brought the smell of flowers across the yard. After the wind had trembled the tall grass, I'd say, "What kind of smell does the wind bring, Uncle Dave?"

"Honeysuckle," he'd answer. "See the vines at the foot of the rocks." The smell would be honeysuckle and the vines were sure enough at the foot of the rocks.

"What does the wind bring now?" I would ask again.

"Wild daisies from right here in the yard," he would answer.

I judged Uncle Dave to be about the smartest man in the valley, and I told him so. He reared back in the split-bottomed chair and said, "Now let me just see about that..." and he stroked his long beard. "What grade are you in at school?"

"Fourth," I said.

"Reckon you got me skinned then," he answered, rubbing his chin. "Not too bad, though. Got me beat by, let's see . . . 'round four, I'd say." And he reared back and laughed again.

Uncle Dave could see better with his eyes closed than any man alive. Mom and Dad and my three brothers and four sisters would hardly be gone before he'd walk into the cabin and come back out with his fiddle under his arm. He'd lift the fiddle to his chin, and I'd sit waiting for his long beard to get caught in the strings, though it never did. "Man that play a fiddle by sight," Uncle Dave said, "ain't fittin' to hold a bow in his hand. Music should be inside you. You got to feel it through your body till it runs down your fingers and comes out the tips onto the strings. If you feel this, you know where to put your fingers. Lord, what company this fiddle is to your Uncle Dave!" And he'd draw the bow and sing with a quivering old voice:

"Give me the flowers while I live,
Trying to cheer me on.
Useless are flowers that you give
After the soul is gone."

Once while Uncle Dave was playing this song I sneaked away from the porch and clipped a handful of wild daisies and brought them to him. And as he took them I watched his closed eyelids quiver, and a tear came from one eye. It scared me at first because I did not know that a blind man could cry; I thought his eyes were sealed so that nothing could come out. And Uncle Dave reared back in the chair and raised the bow again:

"Sweet bunch of daisies
Picked from the dell;
Whisper you love me,
Daisies won't tell."

And one summer while I sat with Uncle Dave on the porch he reached out and touched me. I felt his fingers run through my hair and they crossed the creases of my skin. "I can't see you, Billy," he said. "But you're a Hewlett, I'd say. Spittin' image. A Hewlett 'cept for size. And there's music in you, too." He grinned. "I can hear you pat-pat your feet

53

on the oak boards of the porch. That's the way I started. When I die I want you to have my fiddle."

I was seven years of schooling ahead of Uncle Dave the summer he died. Uncle Frank sent a boy named Wilfred Curry down the river to tell us. Uncle Frank had given him a dollar to make the trip and Wilfred had stopped on the way and got drunk. Heavy rains were in the valley, and the creek that led to the house was swollen high over the banks and we had to walk the sides of the bank to make it. It was rough walking the six miles and Mom made all of us go in front of her so that she could see if one of us slid down the bank and into the swollen creek.

The damp earth had made the grass in the yard grow tall and the night wind had come to break it over and mat it until you could hardly walk to the porch. Uncle Dave was in a pine coffin that Frank had made. Uncle Dave looked like he had lain down to sleep for a while. His long white beard had been combed and his eyes were still closed.

"Glad you got here," Frank said, as he walked out to meet us. "Dave's been dead three days now. Don't believe I could have kept him overnight. The weather's hot and sulky and he's already begun to turn. I couldn't have made it up the slope with him. That damned Wilfred didn't come back with you? Got drunk instead, I reckon. Well, he was the only soul I could send. Didn't want to leave Dave alone here at the house." I thought that if Uncle Dave could have talked he would have quarreled at Frank for thinking that he needed tending to. "Dave didn't want to be buried in the low ground. Wanted to be on top of the knoll there where the pine tree sets."

I remembered the many times that Uncle Dave had talked about the lone pine on the ridge above the house. Below the pine a small strip of land had been cleared, and while Frank worked the strip he used to lead Uncle Dave up the hill and let him sit under the shade of the pine. High up here the wind blew, and through the needles of the great pine it sang a mournful song.

Uncle Dave had not been born blind. Age had closed his eyes slowly, and shadows and images had remained in front of them for a long period of time. The image of the great pine standing alone on the high ridge with nothing behind it but the sky had been the last to disappear. There was a closeness between him and the tree, and he asked about it often.

"Is it still there?" he would ask. "Is it still there?" And he would sit on the porch looking toward the tree.

Being so near the small patch of corn, the pine tree became a sentry post for the crows that came to eat Frank's corn. By the time I was big enough to come to the hollow, Uncle Dave had learned this. He'd sit on the porch staring toward the tree and say, "How many crows are in the pine?"

"One ... two ... three ..." and other crows would circle and light in the pine and mix me up.

Uncle Dave would know that I was stuttering to count and he would grin and say, "I reckon the crows are settin' 'round the top like petals 'round the center of a daisy, ain't they?"

"Yes."

"Comin' and goin', ain't they?"

"Yes."

"Ain't much use to try and count, then."

And then he'd laugh again and say, "Look in the top of the pine. There's a big, black crow settin' there watching for ole Frank. If Frank tried to sneak up the slope, he'll warn the others that Frank is coming. I could just save that old crow a lot of settin' if I was able to tell him how crooked Frank is with a gun. He could swoop down out of that tree and get his bellyful with the rest."

"But won't he get to eat?" I would ask, staring at the black crow and feeling sorry for him.

"Yes," Uncle Dave said. "Soon a crow'll come out of Frank's corn patch to rest him a spell. This crow will watch for Frank while the other one eats. Now, if I was that crow I'd rather set in the top of that big pine than to eat any time. I could find me something better to look for than Frank." And Uncle Dave would rear back and laugh.

In the end, Uncle Dave's dream came true. He'd sit on the knoll like the sentry crow overlooking the valley. He'd be high on the ridge where the wind made a strange noise through the needles of the lone pine tree. A fiddle tune that Uncle Dave often played went like this:

> "'Neath the pine, 'neath the pine
> Where the sun will never shine,
> Winds whisper and the cold wind blows."

That evening, as we walked down the creek out of the hollow, I thought only of the fiddle Uncle Dave had promised me when he died. I begged Mom to let me go back to the house and get the fiddle so that I could take it home with me. "It's not fitting to take a man's belongings before the sun has set over his grave," Mom said.

The sun rose and set many times. People that had never bothered to sit and talk with Uncle Dave came to plunder his belongings. They took the fiddle. But they wouldn't be apt to get away with taking it, I thought. It was a bad omen, Mom said, to take from the dead what you had not been welcomed to before. And I believed her.

iv

A picture of Grandpa Clark hung on the wall at home, and I often stared at it. Grandpa Clark was tall and lean as a sapling but the picture seemed to jam him up like the closing of an accordion. His hair was as black as a seam of coal and he wore a great handle-bar mustache, casting a shadow over his pointed chin.

Grandpa Clark had worked his life away as a coal miner. Before he was twelve years old, he traveled the hillsides early of the morning before daylight when the grass was dewy enough to wet his clothes to the skin. Somewhere along the slopes, he would duck into a black pocket where daylight would never break. The coal mines he worked were the small belly mines of the valley, so narrow that, once inside, he could not turn around. To leave the mine he had to back out, guiding himself with his hand, touching the black walls on either side.

Now and then he'd feel a large mine rat on his legs, and he'd lie flat until it crossed his head and disappeared farther into the mine. These rats grew to enormous size, and they were extremely vicious. But, although Grandpa Clark feared and hated the mine rats, he admired them for their cunning, and he carried tall tales about the rats from mine to mine. In his day, the mine lamps burned lard oil. Grandpa Clark claimed that the rats were smart enough to coil their long tails around the caps on the lamp bowls and unscrew them. Then, sticking their tails into the open hole, they would dip out the oil and lick it from their tails until he was left in darkness.

He lay on his side until it became numb, pecking with a miners' pick at the black seams of coal over his head, closing his eyes as the coal broke loose, to keep the dust from blinding him. After he'd picked a while, he gathered the coal chunks in a burlap sack and backed out of the mine, pulling the sack with him. And he'd grab a gulp of fresh air and weave back through the mine like a long, lean blacksnake, twisting and bending to follow the seam of coal.

Dad was the only boy of his family. When he was ten years old, he went with Grandpa Clark to dig coal.

During his many years of twisting, pecking, and dragging, Grandpa Clark had one dream: someday he would buy a small strip of land here in the valley and build a home. A man must be rooted to home, he believed. No roots made a wanderer's foot. Through the years, he managed to save a hundred dollars and with this and a fine team of white mules he traded for fifty acres of land. This was a happy day for him. Now he worked nights, when he was free from the mines, building his home.

He had divided his family among friends until the house was livable. Only Dad remained with him. Dad could be a great help in cutting trees and clearing a patch for a garden. During the warm summer nights, they slept out on the open hillside with the sky for a roof and the tall grass to tuck around them if the wind became keen. When the rains came, they sheltered under the many rock cliffs here in the valley. Before the winter had passed one room of the home was completed, and Grandpa Clark and Dad spent the cold nights inside. Spring came. Then Summer. The house had four rooms, enough to bring the family together again.

But before he could gather them up, he was served an eviction notice. Bunt Borders, with whom Grandpa Clark had made the trade, claimed that Grandpa Clark had swapped him two sick mules and had failed to pay the hundred dollars. Grandpa Clark knew better. The white mules had been great workers, the best he had ever owned. For a man like Bunt Borders, they had nearly killed themselves. Hitched onto too many logs for a load, they sunk their hoofs into the clay of the hills and, with froth running from their mouths and foamy sweat dripping from their sides, they burst their guts out trying to move.

"Do you have receipts to show that you paid him the hundred dollars or that both mules were sound?" the constable asked.

"I have my word," Grandpa Clark said. "That ought to be enough for any man."

"It won't be enough in the courts against an important man like Bunt Borders," the constable said. "You'll have to prove it in court."

"If the time has come when a man's word is no good

and honesty won't stand against a common thief, there's little use of my going to courts," said Grandpa Clark. And since his only deed had been a final handshake and a belief that a man's word was his deed, he left the land.

"Poor Richard Clark," I heard Mom say many times. "Humbling and honest and cheated to the grave. Only rest he ever found was the day they covered his coffin. Never even owned the land he was buried on. Your dad paid for it when times were hard, and it took food from the table."

v

Grandma Clark spent the last years of her life here in the valley living for periods of time with each of her five children. She came to our house each year when the leaves had darkened on the trees and the pawpaws had ripened. Of the fall, I used to sit and watch for her to come down the path, around the side of the hill to our house. From a distance I could see her long gray hair tied in a bun, as she turned her head from side to side. Grandma Clark's skin was as dark as an autumn leaf and she was not much taller than the handle of a gooseneck hoe. She knew that the pawpaws were ripe again, and she had come here to eat them, I thought. She came also to share her small pension check that she received from the government. While she remained with us, she would try to pay at least part of her way and not take badly needed food from the table.

Her check amounted to only a few dollars. Dad's share

was never more than a dollar, and he didn't want to take it from her. But Grandma Clark would have it no other way and she would catch Dad with his head turned and sneak a folded dollar bill into his pocket. This used to worry me a great deal. Sometimes she wouldn't push the dollar bill all the way into his pocket and Dad, sort of pretending the dollar was not there at all, would walk around the house paying no attention to it. I used to follow him around, watching his pocket and the dollar bill, thinking that it might fall from his pocket. But sometime during the day Dad always managed to pull the dollar from his pocket and hand it over to Mom.

First thing Grandma Clark would say when she came was "Run to the pawpaw patch, honey, and fetch your granny a ripened pawpaw."

"Already fetched 'em," I'd say, pointing toward the roof of the small outhouse where I had placed them.

"Bless my soul if you ain't," she'd say, squinting her little narrow eyes. "Shinny to the top and bring me the one that the frost has turned the yellowest. That one will be the ripest. Your old granny'd be apt to starve if she had to climb all that way herself."

Grandma Clark was almost full-blooded Shawnee Indian and her features told it: dark skin, narrow eyes with crow's feet, and high cheekbones. She knew the hills better than most men of the valley. She knew the herb roots, where they grew, and what they would cure. When one of us took sick, it was Grandma Clark who found the cure. She walked into the hills and gathered yellow root, poke root, mayapple, peppermint, tea leaves, sassafras, and many others.

She knew how to make the poultice to take down swelling from falls or snake bites. Some she made with the leaves of the plantain green, others with a slice of raw potato, the white skin from the shell of an egg, onions, or the fat from the side of a hog. A wad of chewing tobacco would hold down infection.

And if the cure for the sickness wasn't to be found in the herbs of the hills, she knew where else to look. For instance, my younger sister Mary came down with the thrush. There were no herb roots to cure this. Grandma Clark made ready for a trip almost five miles up the head of a hollow, to the small cabin where Blind Tom lived. Blind Tom had been blessed with the power of calling one of the greatest of all spirits of the hills, the "Knocking Spirit." If a believer in the power of this spirit came down with a sickness that a root herb could not cure, Blind Tom would call forth the spirit and reckon with the sickness. In a case such as the thrush, Blind Tom would rastle with the spirit and then blow down the victim's throat with his own breath.

So now Mary and I set out up the hollow toward Blind Tom's, Grandma Clark leading the way.

Blind Tom lived with an older sister in a small two-room oak-slabbed house. He had a long beard, three-quarters gray, and his eyes were not closed like Uncle Dave's. They were as blue around the edges as the summer sky and the center was as white as the trail a snail leaves across a rock. There was a veil over his eyes, Grandma Clark said. This was not her first visit to Blind Tom's house and he knew her; most important, he knew that Grandma believed in the spirits and signs of the hill country. He reached out, took sister Mary, and pulled her to his lap. She began to cry. I puckered my face and Grandma Clark frowned and raised her finger to her lips for quietness.

"Hush!" Grandma Clark said, trying to soothe Mary. "Hush, now!"

"Do you believe in the Knocking Spirit?" Blind Tom asked, his head bobbing from side to side and his voice rolling out of his beard like low thunder.

"I believe for her," Grandma Clark said. "She is yet too little."

Blind Tom ran his hand over Mary's face until he felt her mouth. He squinted his eyes and looked off in the direction of the hills.

"Listen!" he said. "The Knocking Spirit comes!" And the pop-pop-popping of the limbs of the trees brushing together outside the house drifted louder in the quietness. Blind Tom bent low and blew his breath into Mary's mouth and he mumbled queer words, sounding like nothing I had ever heard. "Whoo-e-e-e... They come! The spirits is among us!"

I snuggled up to Grandma Clark, just about as close as I could get, and I shivered as if all the winds of winter had gathered and trailed down my shirt collar. Blind Tom was now rolling his head from side to side, around and around. Suddenly he stopped. He handed my sister back to Grandma Clark and cocked his ear to the sound of our footsteps as we walked across the yard.

"What did he say, Grandma?" I asked, when I figured we were far enough away for him not to hear.

"Hush!" Grandma Clark said. "You'll cause the spirit to leave the child's mouth before the thrush is gone. It's not for us to know the doings of the Knocking Spirit." And then Grandma Clark became as quiet as the hills of the evening when the sun has set. She knew and believed the spirits, but would not talk of them.

In the days that followed the visit to Blind Tom's, I thought of nothing except the Knocking Spirit. Not only did I think of it, but I became determined that I would try to call and talk with it myself. After much thought, I decided to choose the daytime to summon it. Although it was generally agreed that nights were by far the best time to seek any spirit, daylight offered many advantages to me: I was much faster on my feet during the daylight hours, and besides my nerve was considerably stronger then, too.

Shopescreek, a half hound and half cur that belonged to my brother Jerry, became my victim. Seeing no one in sight one evening, I knelt under a tree in the yard and called him. He came to me with his head down and wagging his tail for all that was in him. Once he was within reach I grabbed him quickly and pulled his jaws apart, and around and around went my head and I did not even know the words I began to mumble to him. And then I said, "Do you believe in the Knocking Spirit, Shopescreek?"

Shopescreek whined and pulled to get away.

"Well, then," I said to him, "since you are a dog I'll believe for you. Listen!" For some reason about now the wind seemed to be keener in the trees and I became a little scared myself. "Do you hear it?"

Shopescreek whined again. I yanked his jaws apart

and blew down his mouth, mumbling words foreign to us both. He twisted his head and looked up at me with sad eyes as if he were trying to figure out what I was saying to him. And then he lowered his nose and sneezed just as any dog will do if you blow down his mouth.

"Listen!" I said again.

Shopescreek began to wag his tail as if something were coming. I became scared. An arm reached down and grabbed me. As quick as I could catch my breath, I tried to run. Mom pulled me high into the air.

Sure enough, this day I heard the Knocking Spirit. But it wasn't the same spirit that Blind Tom knew; it was the knocking of a sprout across my legs. When it came to fearing mockery of the spirits, Mom was equal to Grandma Clark.

"Lord!" Grandma Clark said, "mockery of the spirits is the worst of all omens!" Mom walloped me again and shook her head in agreement.

You'll gather that pawpaw yourself tomorrow, Grandma Clark, I thought, as welts rose on my legs. The extra lick you got me today will cost you pawpaws tomorrow.

Camden's Interstate Street Car Company's bridge crossing the Big Sandy River, Catlettsburg.

"On the day that I was born here in the valley, my mother crossed the Big Sandy River from Catlettsburg by streetcar to Huntington, West Virginia, which was ten miles away."

CHAPTER 4

On the day that I was born here in the valley, my mother crossed the Big Sandy River from Catlettsburg by streetcar to Huntington, West Virginia, which was ten miles away. This was the farthest distance that Mom ever ventured from home. When she crossed the Big Sandy Bridge, she always closed her eyes, caught her breath, and prayed that the bridge wouldn't fall—at least not until she reached Kentucky soil again. For the bargains she could find in Huntington, she was willing to take her chance with the bridge and the streetcar.

This day she was buying used clothing for the family. Winter was deep in the valley and the clothing of the family was about as thin as it would wear without breaking through. There were used-clothing stores in Catlettsburg too, but used clothing bought in Huntington was less likely to be recognized in Catlettsburg. The fact was, my oldest brother James had come home from school the day before screaming with all the might he could muster. A boy in his grade at school had recognized a pair of knickers James was wearing as a pair that he had once owned and his mother had donated to the last drive of the Younger Women's Society of Catlettsburg.

"You're a liar!" James said to him, setting his feet solid in the schoolyard dust and challenging him to a fist fight. The boy would not fight James, but since he and James argued so loud, a crowd gathered around them. James denied that the knickers had been bought at the rummage sale. He made tall tales of where Mom had purchased them, naming the best store in Catlettsburg. He bragged so loud that when the boy challenged him to look inside the knickers near the waist, he had to look, praying that the laundry initials would not be there. So James turned the waist of the pants and all eyes of the crowd looked with him. And there, scribbled in black letters, were the initials "B.M." And, faster than a weasel could skin out of a brush pile along the banks of Catlettscreek, James was out of the schoolhouse yard, and he didn't stop till he reached the house. That evening the word spread to the rest of the family. And they all huddled together in a circle peeling off their used clothing, while Mom tried to keep them from exposing their nakedness.

So Mom traveled over to Huntington, looking for clothes that wouldn't be recognized near home. She had been inside a second-hand store when her first pains of labor came. Quickly gathering up the clothes she had bought, she turned her eyes toward the Big Sandy. One thought occupied her mind: she must make it to Kentucky soil. Once she had reached the Kentucky side of the river, I could be born anywhere.

The streetcar was rough riding and the bumps in the road brought more pains. As Mom gritted her teeth and frowned and searched for the Big Sandy, the driver glanced over at her.

"Something wrong, lady?" he asked as he stopped the streetcar to let a passenger off.

"I'm going to have a baby," Mom said.

"Hell's afire, lady!" the driver yelled. "Not here in the

streetcar! Hold it! Hold it!"

"How far till we cross the Big Sandy?" Mom asked.

"Not far," the driver answered. "How far do you live from the end of the bridge?"

"Below the mouth of Catlettscreek," Mom said.

"Then, great God, hold off till we get there, lady!"

He slammed the door and pushed the streetcar as fast as it would go. And the rest of the passengers on the car hollered and quarreled as the driver passed their stops, refusing to let them off. And now and then he looked over at Mom, "Hold it, lady! Hold it just a little longer!"

The thought of risking her life bothered Mom far less than the fact that if we did not make it across the Big Sandy I would be born a "foreigner."

The river came into sight. The waters were swelling quickly now and rising over the banks. Mom didn't notice, and neither did the driver.

Reaching the Kentucky side of the river, he hollered, "Where now, lady?" sweat dripping from his face.

"Just the other side of the creek," Mom answered. And as she walked in the front door of our home the water from the two rivers was rising onto the back porch. Dad ran from the house and brought a doctor back with him. Then Dad paced the floor, while the doctor kept one eye on Mom and one eye on the rivers, already coming in the back door.

"It's even chances which will come first, the baby or the rivers," he said to Dad.

Mom could not be moved now. And even if she could be, there was only one place she could be taken: the small grade school that stood high on the hillside at the other side

Division Street during high water, Catlettsburg.

"The waters were swelling quickly now and rising over the banks."

of town. The pains kept coming and just as the men had reached a decision to try to make it to the schoolhouse the pains became real close.

And with a foot of water in the house, the bed where Mom lay surrounded by the waters of the two rivers, I was born, in the rivers of the valley.

An hour later she was taken from the house in a joeboat, Dad sitting in one end holding me in his arms and Mom and the rest of the family huddled in the center, leaving hardly enough room to oar.

"The schoolhouse is not a fitting place to take a baby less than two hours old," Dad said as the joeboat skimmed across the muddy water. And less than forty yards from where our former home was now bobbing in the muddy water, he passed a large two-story house, and, seeing people leaving it, a thought came to him. He sized the house up. It was an old building and leaned like an old willow tree. The people that lived in it had carried out their last belongings and Brice Flanners, the owner, was standing there watching to see if the current would lift the house from its foundations and carry it down river. This was one of the many old buildings that Brice Flanners owned in town. Most of them weren't fit to live in, but still they were rented by people like us, who could afford no better.

When the joeboat reached the bank, Dad stepped out on land and walked up to him.

"Want to rent that house?"

"Right now?" Brice Flanners said.

"The way it stands now," Dad answered.

"Well, it's empty," he said. "I'll lease it."

71

"How much?" Dad asked.

"A hundred dollars for the year," Brice Flanners said.

"A hundred dollars!" Dad said. "I don't have that kind of money."

"You have shoe machinery," Brice Flanners said. "I'll take a mortgage on that."

"Well, it's a bargain," Dad said.

And so before I was ever on land, the joeboat was turned into the current again and Dad set the family one at a time on the steps leading to the upstairs of the house.

On the second floor the family gathered to watch the rivers and Dad paced the floor, looking down the long rows of steps, gauging how far the water had crept up. Dad was taking one of the biggest gambles of his life. People stood on the banks waiting to see who would win, Dad or the rivers. But Dad knew these waters; few men knew them better. And a grin came to his face. He had rented the house at less than one third of what Brice Flanners had been getting for it. Brice Flanners was not a man to give anything away, especially money—but he'd been running from these rivers too long to know them.

Sure enough, two days after we rented the house the rivers were back within their banks. The family crept down the steps, shoving the mud back into the water where it came from. They built a fire inside the first floor to dry the wood out quickly, so the sun and weather would not warp it any worse.

Everyone in Catlettsburg was familiar with the "Leaning Tower" house. Most all of them had come at one time or another to stare at it, sure that someday the wind would blow it the rest of the way over. They stood there watching, thinking it might fall before their eyes. The younger people of the town came too. They poked fun and dared each other to lean against the bent side of the house. Most who took the dare were sure that the house would tumble and leave them as flat as a Skipjack. Mom complained of the house. Unless she blocked her furniture, she said, the pieces would move around the rooms as if motors were attached to them.

The old house had stood against many floods here in the valley. Most of the houses that could have matched it in age had long ago been lost to the rivers. Its boards inside and out were warped by time and the rivers. In the summer, small trees sprouted all along the roof, their seeds brought by the wind and sowed in the black muck the rivers had deposited high in the gutters.

By the time I was old enough to know that it was supposed to be leaning, I had lived at an angle so long that I didn't have good judgment of straight and crooked. Even so, this would have taken nothing away from the house as far as I was concerned. Being set close to the rivers made it a mansion. The rivers surrounding it made it a shantyboat too, which at the time seemed to me even greater than a mansion.

If you could take the greenness of the willow leaf, reach

Big Sandy River, near Catlettsburg.
Photo courtesy of Billy C. Clark

"If you could take the greeness of the willow leaf, reach up
and pull the blue from a summer sky, and mix them together,
you would have had the normal color the two rivers held.

up and pull the blue from a summer sky, and mix them together, you would have had the normal color the two rivers held. Each river was practically within rock-throwing distance of the house. If this wasn't enough, Catlettscreek wound out of the hill and emptied close enough to the Leaning Tower that you could spit in it. By the time I was seven years old, I had learned many things from these rivers.

I knew about the seasons of the year. Spring brought leaves along the willow-tree limbs as thick as the grains of sand along the banks. Summer warmed the sand banks deeper than I could sink a toe into them. Autumn blew brown leaves along the surfaces of the rivers, quilting them as far out as the currents would allow without taking them down river. Ducks came over the rivers in great V formations. A few scattered geese honked, and men gathered along the banks and shot at them with rifles and shotguns. Now and then one would fall and the hunter would hurry to the willow grove to strip off his clothing. He knew that along the edges of the rivers, hunkered like a bullfrog ready to jump, a boy already naked to the skin would most likely beat him out to the fallen bird.

The boy was fast in the rivers and on land too. And he held another advantage on land: naked boys did not hesitate to go near the town where people would stare at them, while a man could be put in jail for it. The Younger Women's Society had long ago complained of all of us swimming in the rivers naked—but the police were like the rivers of the summer, too slow and lazy to catch a field mouse. We ate more ducks and geese of the autumn than any family in Catlettsburg without firing a shot.

Of the autumn, I often sat at the mouth of Catlettscreek waiting for the big mallards to swing around the bend in the Ohio and nose into the creek, on their way to rob Melvin Bigsby's corn fields deeper into the hills. Sometimes a hunter would pull up in a joeboat and say to me, "Any ducks go up this creek, boy?"

"Nope," I'd say, thinking that the ducks had more of a right to the rivers than the hunter. The duck was a dog paddler, and I had a softness for dog paddlers.

Winter brought loneliness to the rivers. The wind blew from the hills and swept down the banks, rattling the limbs of the willow, maple, sycamore, and water birch with a song more mournful than a mountain ballad from Dad's fiddle. The trees were naked, and many of them were bent like the backs of old people here in the valley who came to the river to fish for catfish. In the forks of all the trees old leaves hung and rattled in the wind, glued to the forks by river muck. Brown circles were on the trunks of every tree, recording the moods of the rivers.

Boats often came up and down the bigger river. In warm weather, the older boys of the town loved to swim to the center and catch the first waves off the bucket boards of the paddle wheels.

Of all the boats that traveled the Ohio, the *Tom Green* was the mightiest. The pull of the *Tom Green* could almost suck you from the bank, or if you were out in the river it could wash you high on the sand. If I could ever swim to the center of the Ohio and take the rollers of the *Tom Green*, I felt I would be in the class with all the older boys that traveled the rivers.

I sat for days on end not big enough to swim to the

center of the big river. At the age of five, I was known on the river as a "mud crawler"—that is, big enough to go into the river but too small to remain afloat. In the shallow edges of the river, a mud crawler supported himself by touching bottom with his hands and pulling himself along. Only his dreams could take him to the center of the river.

At the age of six I graduated to being a "dog paddler." Then I thought I had the big river licked. I planned to swim out and take the rollers of the Tom Green. I waited days for the big boat to come up river. Shadows along the river caught me still waiting, but the Tom Green did not come. Maybe it's because the rivers are low, I thought, and the big Tom Green can't draw enough water. Then one day I overheard an older boy say, "Hear about the Tom Green? Took her from the Ohio. Too big. She was washing the small boats up on the bank and tearing joeboats loose from the willows. Gone to the Mississippi."

Ohio River steamboat, near Ashland.

"...boys of the town loved to swim to the center of the river and catch the first waves off the bucket boards of the paddle wheels."

Bertha Hewlett Clark.
My mom's heart was as free as the waters of the Big Sandy.

Mason Clark.
My dad's lonesome fiddle sung as sweet as a mountain wind.
Photo courtesy of Billy C. Clark.

"I don't know why your dad would want to lie to you about his schooling. He well knows that he went only as far as the first grade, and I went through the second."

CHAPTER 5

Dad claimed that he had gone as far as the second grade before he had to quit school and go to work and help his family. Mom overheard him, and when he had left the house for work that day she said to me: "I don't know why your dad would want to lie to you kids about his schooling. He well knows that he went only as far as the first grade, and I went through the second. Ask him who taught him to write his name."

My brother Jerry had just entered the second grade. It seemed to me that he had done just about the greatest thing possible to do. Before he'd had his first haircut, he had beaten Dad in school. How bad I wanted to get started toward beating Dad's record myself!

Each morning I watched my three brothers pout because they had to walk to school with my two older sisters. They left the house before the fog had lifted from the rivers, James in front with his bowl haircut, Bob and Jerry with their hair still to their shoulders like the girls. Some mornings I trailed along behind them, but they always caught me before we reached the schoolhouse, and James brought me back.

"Hush now!" Mom would say. "You'll soon be big enough to go and when you do you'll beat them all. You'll see." I'd learned one thing about Mom from Dad: there was no use whatsoever arguing with her.

I wish you could have known my mother. She was short and squatty, her face wind-tanned and a few streaks of black remaining among the many gray hairs. During the days, now I went with her, leading my two younger sisters, while she gathered clothes from house to house to bring back home to wash. Then she washed the clothes over a washboard until her hands would turn as red as the feathers of the redbird that roosted in the willows along the rivers at night. The skin would split and the blood would seep from the cracks and she would stop long enough to rub her hands in baking flour to keep them from bleeding. Mom would not quit. I felt sorry for her and often wanted to help her rub the clothes over the washboard.

"You just watch after your sisters and the tub of water on the stove," she would say. "That'll be a man's job."

When the clothes were all washed, we would take them to the back of the Leaning Tower and hang them on a wire line. The breeze that came from the rivers dried them quickly. I followed along after her, trying to help lift the heavy basket of wet clothes. But I couldn't, and I settled for handing her each piece and clothespins to hold it on the line. I had a feeling that I was helping to earn money to pay bills at the house and put food on the table.

There were many other things Mom could do to earn money with her hands. She could take an old piece of furniture and scrape, tack, and sew it and make it look new. She would sell any piece of furniture in the house any time—or she'd give it away just as quickly if it were bragged about. Mom often gave to needier families. Her heart was as big and broad as the great Ohio River.

"She'll give away a chair with someone setting in it," Dad often said.

Salesmen came to the Leaning Tower, and Mom bought whatever they had. Their long sales talks were a waste of breath, because Mom was eager to buy anything they peddled. Word spread, and more came, each charging Mom an outlandish price on credit.

But she outsold them all. They left by the front door and Mom left by the back. Carrying their wares around, she sold to people for half what she had signed her name for. When the salesman came to collect, she was never home. "Run to the door, Billy," she'd say. "Tell them I'm not here."

It was Dad's belief that if Mom did not eventually give the house away, her cats would take over. Mom's theory was that the cats she owned had been sent to her as a blessing to cope with the river rats that came of the nights to the Leaning Tower to scratch over the floor, tables, beds, and everything else in the house, leaving their mud prints to show where they had been. They were big, many the size of half-grown cats.

There must have been hundreds of stray cats in Catlettsburg, and not one missed the Leaning Tower for his lunch. They did not feast on rats. Dad reckoned that there wasn't a cat in the lot with enough guts to tackle a rat. Many of the cats remained with us permanently, with Mom humoring them and treating them like members of the family. My brothers hid under the willows and conked them with river gravel, and once they tied two big toms' tails together and hung them over a low branch and they fought until they died.

As if the stray cats were not enough to contend with, my sisters carried sacks of kittens from the creek where people had thrown them. The kittens would be soaked with water and mud and usually so small that their eyes were not yet opened.

"Poor things," Mom would say, and she'd wipe them off and put them in the bread pan, then shove them into the oven under a slow heat to revive them.

The cats had as many breeds in them as Chow Burton. Yet to Mom they were all pure Persians, like the big Persian cat that belonged to one of the houses where we gathered clothes every week. True, the hair on the cats was as slick as a muskrat slide. But Mom said they were all "just shedding."

They gathered around the table while we ate. Out of the ten of us, they chose Dad as the most likely to feed them. They couldn't have been more wrong! Those cats gathered at his feet and meowed louder than boat whistles on the rivers. They pulled at his pants and sometimes clawed him. But if Dad knocked one to the floor, Mom would have us all frowning at his brutality.

ii

Elza Harkins was our down-river neighbor, known as Clothesline Harkins. The people on the low side of the rivers had given him this nickname, and it stuck.

One day a neighbor had accused him of stealing a clothesline to use as one of the trotlines he stretched from a snag at the mouth of Catlettscreek out into the big Ohio and anchored with a large river rock. It was a bad mistake to accuse Elza Harkins of stealing, either rightly or wrongly. He was a huge man with bushy hair that didn't stop growing on his head but sprouted just as thick over his back and chest and down his arms to the tips of his fingers. The few times I heard him speak his voice rolled out as if it had been piped through a hollow log. His arms hung to his side and swung back and forth when he walked as if they were on ball bearings.

"I've traced you to it, Elza," Ulyss Paddler said the day he faced Elza by the rivers. Ulyss's head reached to Elza's shoulders, with Ulyss standing on the high side of the bank. "I know you took the clothesline. Ain't no other man in this valley could leave a set of prints beside the post like that. You're a bigger man than me, but I ain't sittin' back and have you steal that line, with rope as high as it is at the hardware store."

Big Elza reached out with a gooseneck hoe that he was using to weed a strip of garden, hooked Ulyss behind the neck with it and drew him up like pulling in a fishing line. "I'll make fish bait out of you!" he said. Then he laid the hoe aside.

But Big Elza tore into a buzzsaw. Ulyss weaved in and out of his arms like a minnow through the holes in a fish trap. And each time he came out he poked Elza in the gut. Now and then Big Elza would strike a glancing blow and Ulyss would go sprawling in the sand. But by the time Elza could reach the spot where Ulyss had rolled, Ulyss was on his feet again, moving around to tap Elza in the back of the head with a blow that didn't have force enough to knock the pinchers from a crawdad.

"You little son of a bitch!" Big Elza hollered. "You've poked me with them little sweat-bee stings of yours till I'm mad enough to bite the bucket boards off a paddle wheel. I'll render you down till you're no bigger'n a cracklin'."

The sun had been directly overhead when the fight had started, but by now it had moved until it touched the Ohio banks. Both men staggered back and forth, drunk from the heat of the sun, and Ulyss reached out as Big Elza stooped to wipe the sweat from his head and pulled huge gobs of hair out by the handfuls. Moving so much weight around in the sun had withered Elza. Ulyss became cocky. He moved in with his sweat-bee blows and came back out. Each time he backed he was closer to the edge of the river. At last he staggered too close and his feet set solid in mud. He squirmed to get free and sank to his knees. Big Elza felled him in one blow. And he sat down on Ulyss and sunk him farther down in the mud until only his head showed. Blowing the river mud from his lips, Ulyss looked up and said, "I fit you Big Elza. I'm whupped. Bein' that I couldn't whup you to get back the line, the least you can do is offer me a mess of fish from it now and then."

Right from the beginning, I was suspicious of Clothesline Elza. I was always afraid that he might set his eyes and take a notion to make a trotline out of our clothesline. Then Dad might become mad and take his "equalizer" and go hunting for Clothesline. The "equalizer" was a forty-four pistol that Dad kept under his pillow at nights.

James, Bob, and Jerry could swim both rivers at one time by first crossing the mouth of the Big Sandy, circling the West Virginia point, and then on across the big Ohio.

While they swam to the Ohio bank, I dog-paddled across the mouth of Catlettscreek, with my eyes closed making believe that it was the big river I was crossing.

Dog-paddling the creek was not much fun. I ate up the distance too quickly for a good-sized dream to develop. Then I sat on the banks and watched my brothers swim to the center of the Ohio to take the rollers from the *Gordon C. Green*. I could hear the men on deck cursing and warning my brothers to stay away from the giant paddle wheels. But into the first rollers they went, like three muskrats after an ear of drift corn. They bobbed up and down in the giant waves, high into the air and then buried between two rollers. And, disgusted to think that I might never get to take rollers of the *Gordon C.*, I dog-paddled far enough into the big Ohio to reach the waves.

I watched my brothers stand here under the willows on the Kentucky shore and holler across the Ohio at boys on the far bank. "Buckeye knockers!" they yelled over and shook their fists.

"Corn crackers!" the Ohioans yelled back, their voices rolling over the water like waves.

I would stand by myself and holler across the river at boys, and I would frown and shake my fists for all that was in me. "Buckeye knockers!"

But no answer came back across the river. My voice was high and shrill and it died along the surface of the great river without strength to cross. But still I hollered, hoping each time that my voice would make it.

The leaves grew thicker on the willow, birch, maple, and sycamore, and the brown balls of the sycamore fell and new green ones replaced them. Now the boats came more often, and the churn of the paddle wheel swelled out in waves over the river, and the smoke from the stack trailed off with the wind. If the day was clear, the smoke rose high above the trees and the wind thinned it out. But when the clouds were heavy and dark, the smoke huddled over the river so close that if you were floating on your back you could have reached up and poked your hand through it.

The kingfisher, sandpiper, killdeer, catbird, redbird, thrush, sparrow, and dove searched the brush along the banks for food, keeping one eye open for boys, deadeyes with rocks.

Early of the summer the two rivers rose and pushed water deep into the creeks, and the big fish swam up the smaller streams to lay eggs and guard them until they hatched and the minnows were alive in the water.

Later in the year the minnows grew. They were called chubs, and they came out to swim in the big rivers. Now they gathered in schools so thick you could catch two at a time on a line rigged with two nib hooks. The gars and skipjacks came to chase them, breaking the surface here and there to catch a chub that had leaped from the river to dodge them.

When the water moved back out of the creek, it moved almost overnight, and I gathered with my brothers and other boys at the mouth of Catlettscreek. The water from the creek carried silt with it and it built up a bar at the mouth, where the water was so shallow that many of the big fish could not make it back to the river. They gathered here in the pool behind the bar. They were mostly carp and weighed as

Division Street, Catlettsburg.

"No one in town would buy carp to eat."

much as fifteen and twenty pounds, and their fins stuck out of the water as they wiggled back and forth in the shallow water trying to make it across the bar. We would wade through the water, sinking into mud up to our knees, and jump on the back of one of the carp and ride him until he stuck in the mud. Then one of the bigger boys would reach his hand down and slide it through the gills of the large fish and another boy would pull him to shore with a willow fork.

No one in town would buy carp to eat. The word was that a carp was a dirty fish, living on what came out of the sewers that emptied into the rivers. The only way to sell a carp was to find someone that didn't require you to clean the fish while they watched; you cut it up and sold it to them for catfish.

There was plenty to eat of the summer. This is the one season I remember having almost enough to eat. Corn was raised along the river, and I sneaked into the patches at night and pulled ears from the stalks. Then I boiled them in a bucket of river water over a wood fire and ate all I could hold. I roasted minnows on sticks over fires during the days. If you had a good throwing arm you could knock a turtle off a log. Eating roast turtle was living high on the hog. The bullfrog was also choice and of the nights he came out to court along the banks and you could blind him with a light and snatch him with your hands and roast him too on a stick. But the meat of the bullfrog had to be eaten while it was hot. Allow it to cool, and the meat was as raw as it had been when you had slipped the skin from him.

The latter part of the summer was watermelon time. Few watermelons were raised in the narrow strips of land on the Kentucky side, so you had to travel across to Ohio to get them. Over in the Ohio country the level land stretched a half day's walk from the edge of the river.

During the days, now my brothers crossed the Ohio River to the watermelon patches. I stood on the Kentucky side watching them sneak up the far banks into the willows, looking so small that I could have strung them over a fishing hook. My job was to wait and watch for Mom to come down the banks. If she came, my signal was to shinny up the tallest willow and wave a big red handkerchief.

I watched them sneak back out of the willows, the big melon rolling in front of them. Sometimes a man would come just behind them and he'd stop at the edge of the river and curse them, and if my voice traveled across the river as loud as his I could have called everyone in Ohio a buckeye knocker and they'd have heard me.

They swam toward the Kentucky shore pushing the big melon in front of them, and the melon would be bobbing up and down and I would hold my breath and pray that it wouldn't sink. They came into shallow water and rolled the melon up on the bank. And we pulled willow leaves and made a green table of them in the shade, and under the trees the melon was broken open and divided. I always got more rind than red melon and, while my brothers stretched out to sleep, like you will when you have too much melon to eat, I stretched out with the bellyache from green rinds.

But the day would come, I thought, when I would cross the river and bring back my own melon, and then I would sit here under the willows and eat until my belly was as full as a river chub and I would stretch out to sleep just like my brothers.

Just across the river was perhaps the best watermelon patch to be found in Ohio. Willow trees grew almost to the edge of the garden, close enough for a person to stand under the cover of the willows and pick out the melon that he intended to take. The thing to do was to sneak quickly into the patch and conk the side of the melons until the sound came back to you like a hollow log. This was a sure sign that the watermelon was ripe.

Every day now I eyed the distance across the river. It was a long way, even with a log.

But not far from our house, Clothesline Elza's lone watermelon vine grew. There had been two melons on the vine earlier in the summer, but blight had touched one and it had rotted out. There was only one left now and almost every day Clothesline Elza came to look at it. He would bend his huge body over the little melon and curl his finger and conk it and turn his face to listen to the sound. And sometimes I would be sitting under the willows high on the bank, a clear sight down to the melon. Earlier of the summer he had only given me mean looks; but the melon had been small then. The sun had bulged it fast. And one evening he stopped, looked up at me, and said in a deep voice that seemed to lift the sand from the riverbank, "You better run on home, you little river tramp! Don't you buzzard that melon!"

And so now when I wanted to see the little melon I had to sneak through the willows to do so. And as I did, I could see that I was not the only one coming to look at the melon; tracks were everywhere in the sand leading to the lone vine.

Before the summer was over, my voice carried across the great Ohio River and the answer came back across the water. I was big enough to take a log and get me an Ohio melon. Thinking that it might take a while to cross the river, I planned to do it early of the morning, allowing the fog to lift from the water so that I could see my way and not get run over by a paddle-wheel boat.

I picked out a good dry log on the riverbank and rolled

it into the river and splashed in after it. Grabbing one end of the log I kicked my feet and nosed out into the river, remembering what I had heard my brothers say: when you cross the big river, keep your eye on the Ohio bank. If you look back, you see a bank moving farther away with each stroke, and the distance is apt to scare you.

As I kicked out, I passed the snag sticking from the water at the mouth of Catlettscreek and heard the swirling water around the snag, making a whirlpool that had strength enough to suck small brush into it. What if it pulled me under too, I thought, and I set my eyes on the Ohio banks and churned up water like a paddle-wheel boat. Farther out into the river I went, and I saw the West Virginia point sticking out into the river like a long brown neck of a snapper turtle. What if a turtle, a big turtle, thinks my toes are a string of minnows? I kicked my feet harder. What if a big catfish thinks my legs are a big wiggling worm? I pulled up my legs and straddled the log. But there was a current and I lost distance. I could see the willows on the Ohio banks passing by me and I knew that I would have to risk the turtles and catfish.

I closed my eyes and put my head across the log and kicked until I felt the limbs of the willows brush the top of my head; then I reached up and grabbed them and pulled the log to shore. I stepped out on the bank and pulled one end of the log on land so that it would not float off and leave me.

If I looked back to the Kentucky side of the river I became scared and I knew why my voice had been so long in traveling across. I turned up the bank through the willows.

Brushing the limbs aside, I looked out into the patch behind the red barn. Melons were everywhere and they stretched out in the patch lazy under the sun. Taking a quick glance around, I scooted into the patch. I stopped first at the biggest melon I had spotted from the edge of the willows, but this one was too big for me to handle. I stooped beside a smaller one and curled my finger and conked it, and the hollow sound drifted so loud across the field that I hunkered low in the melon vines, sure it must have been heard. Slowly I twisted the melon's stem and broke it from the vine. And, crawling on my stomach, I pushed it in front of me back to the willows.

At the top of the steep bank the melon got away from me, and before I could get in front of it, it had rolled into the river and disappeared. I held my breath, but up it came and drifted slowly down river. I ran down the bank, pushed the log back into the water, and caught the melon. And with one arm around the melon and one arm around the log, I kicked toward the Kentucky shore.

I had reached about the center of the river and things seemed to be going my way. Then all of a sudden, from below the bend I saw a stream of smoke drift over the willow tops. A boat whistle sounded over the surface of the river and bounced along the banks and the great paddle wheel came into sight. Cold chills came over me as the whistle blew again. I figured that the boat had spotted me and was blowing for me to get out of the way. I kicked with all my might and screamed at the top of my voice that I was moving as fast as I could.

The big paddle wheel pushed a six-barge tow straight

toward me. I imagined the black ends of the barge sucking me under and grinding me up in the bucket boards of the paddle wheel. My legs cramped and I closed my eyes and heard the men on the barges cursing me. The next thing I knew, the paddle wheel was churning water in my face and I could hardly breathe. But I opened my eyes and looked through the film of water and I could see that I was behind the boat, bobbing up and down in the water. And somehow I still held to the melon and the log. Now the waves began to smooth out as the paddle wheel nosed around the bend up river and the smoke from the stack trailed off into the sky.

The boat's waves had helped push me toward the Kentucky shore. I passed the snag in front of the mouth of Catlettscreek and finally my toes touched sand and, rolling the melon in front of me, I stepped out on the bank.

After I caught my breath, I broke the melon with a sharp gravel and ate the red meat inside until I was so full that I could not keep my eyes open. The sun came hotter through the willows. I was tired from the pull across the big river. I stretched out on the sand to sleep.

The next thing I knew someone had me by the arm. I opened my eyes thinking for a minute I was still on the Ohio banks in the watermelon patch and I had been caught. But I blinked my eyes and saw Mom standing over me. Beside her stood Clothesline Elza!

"There's my melon!" Clothesline Elza said, pointing his finger at me. "Look at it! He didn't eat enough to fill a bird's craw. The rest has ruined in the hot sun." The next thing I knew Mom had pulled a switch from a willow and the welts raised on my legs. Up the bank we went, the willow branch coming keener with each step I took.

"I'll have Mason come and pay you for the melon," Mom told him when we reached the house. "I never had one of my boys steal before."

And that night I lay in bed with my eyes swollen and my legs and back holding welts and the skin broken in places. One of my brothers giggled, and then another giggled, and before long they were all giggling. And the smell of watermelon was on their hands.

iii

The greatest thing about the two rivers was that here along the banks there was seldom anyone to stare at you. In town they did. They pointed and laughed at my long hair, which reached to my shoulders and was matted most of the time. When I went up town with Mom I wore knickers. They stared at them too. The knickers I owned were much too big for me and they were patched like the patchwork quilts that Mom made over a wooden frame.

One day here on the rivers, when I was sitting under the willows watching a paddle-wheel boat push a tow up river and thinking how much I'd like to dog-paddle out and take the first breakers from the bucket boards, two men came up the bank toward me.

One of them carried a set of oars over his shoulder and line wound around a wooden stick. The other had a bucket of bait and some trotline nibs strung along a limb.

"Well, looky there, Sim," the one with the oars called

out. "Girl or boy, would you say?" A grin came to his face.

"Girl, ain't it?" his friend answered. "Hair's long like on a girl. Wearin' pants though."

The big man pulled the oars from his shoulders and stuck the blades into the soft sand and rested himself. He twirled the roll of line around in the air.

"Why don't we ask him or her?" he said.

My mouth puckered and I looked down at them.

"I'm a boy!" I said.

"Well!" the big man with the oars said. He rubbed his hand under his chin and looked at me, turning his head from side to side with a grin. Then he drew in his lips. "Don't believe it. Nope. Don't believe it at all. Tell you what, Sim. You jump up there real quick like a cat and snatch him and pull his pants off, and let's me and you see if he's got a turnip stem hangin' down. If he does, I aim to pull the biggest crawdad with the longest pinchers from that bait bucket and let him snip it off to the nubbin'."

Before the man could take a step I was on my feet, and I weaved through the willows faster than a redbird after a flying grasshopper. And, as I ran, my hair flew high into the air and came back down over my face and I kept brushing it off. Tears blinded my sight.

All of a sudden everyone seemed to be staring at my hair and patched clothes. Now I went to the banks of the river and ran my hands through my long hair and tears came to my eyes. I was ashamed of my hair and of my patched clothes. Jerry's hair was as long as mine, but both Bob and James now had bowl haircuts. It seemed to me that my brothers were seasoned to long hair and bowl haircuts the same as a willow tree is seasoned to the weather. They walked along the streets of town and paid little attention to people staring. They had aged to it. But I knew that I never would. If they laughed at me again at school, I thought I would quit.

So I sat under the willows with the cold wind seeping through my clothes, and stared across the water, hoping that a duck would quack up the bank and turn into the creek instead of flying over the West Virginia point and getting shot. I thought of Mom's hands, red from scrubbing clothes on the rough board for other people to wear. And the wind was so cold now that the clothes froze on the line. Maybe, I thought, when she has washed enough clothes, she might just have my hair cut and then it will stay short for at least a little while.

To me there looked to be enough water in these two rivers to wash all the dirt from the face of the earth. Of the fall, the water from the hills drained into the feeder streams and emptied into the rivers and there was more water. The leaves of the willows and maples and birch and sycamore were gone and there was no shade. But it did not matter because there was hardly enough sun to warm the top of the sand. Here on the rivers everything was free. There were no clothes to be washed to pay for the privilege of sitting here watching for the wild ducks and geese to sail in a V overhead, or listening to the wind sing through the naked limbs of the trees. It cost nothing except the walk down the bank.

One day I asked Mom where these beautiful rivers came from. Raising her head from the tub where she was stirring soap slivers, she told me that the two rivers had been put here by God.

I had no knowledge of God and the word confused me. As I rolled the new word over and over my tongue, I was sure of one thing: anyone who could make rivers like the Big Sandy and the Ohio and sprinkle sand banks with trees as pretty as the willows, maples, birch, and sycamore would have to be a great Man.

The more I thought about it, the more I got to wondering, where would such a person live? I did not see His home along the banks of the rivers. I had never passed it in town.

I asked Mom where He lived, this Man with a heart so big that He would give all these things free to a boy with long hair and patched clothes like myself. Mom pointed her finger above the steep ridges of the hills and told me that He lived above the clouds that had come to circle the highest point. I stared toward the hills, less than three hundred yards from the banks of the rivers, and saw the clouds rolling in a great mass, seeming low enough to touch the top of the bony ridge.

"But how could you ever get that far up to thank Him?" I asked.

Mom wiped her hand across her forehead and stared at me.

"Why," she said, "you don't have to go way up there to thank Him. He'd be apt to hear you just as clearly if you was standing under one of them willows you're always talking about."

But still I didn't understand. In the days that followed, I began to stare into the sky above the tops of the willows.

As I stared, I tried to shape His face in the clouds that gathered and trailed off in long paths across the sky. I wondered if He would have long hair like me. When I made out a face in the clouds, I always picked one that had little clouds thinning from it and trailing off to match long locks of hair. Yet it did not seem right to me that a Man this great was not here on the river where a boy could walk up to Him and say, "Thank you."

"Don't God ever come down from the clouds?" I asked Mom one day. "Does He stay up there all the time?"

"Heard He does," Mom said. "He comes down on Sundays now and then."

"Where does He come to?" I asked Mom.

"Well," Mom said, "you know the little brick church that sets near the mouth of the Big Sandy? Well, I s'pose he might come there on Sundays."

"And can I see Him?" I asked.

"Can you see the wind in the trees?" Mom asked.

It was true that I had never been able to see the wind. But many a day when the hot sun had sifted through the trees and burned my shoulders and the sweat had come to my forehead and run down into my face, a wind had swept through the trees and cooled me off. Many times I had dog-paddled around the mouth of the creek and the waves from a paddle wheel had wet my hair and I had stood under the willows, shading my hair into the wind to dry it so that Mom would never know.

"Is church where all the people go when they want to thank Him?" I asked.

"I reckon it might be if you believed you could find

God there," Mom said. I watched her as she rubbed the clothes with her hands. The skin was broken bad in places, and I knew that the lye soap would sting like the touch of salt on an open wound. I had asked so many times to help her.

"You run and play," she would say, "while you're still too young to know troubles."

But I already had troubles. I couldn't understand if God had been to church on Sundays why Mom and Dad and the rest of the family had not gone to thank Him. Dad had once said that his fiddle was the most pleasure that he had on the face of the earth. Why hadn't Dad gone to the church and thanked God for the fiddle that Grandpa Hewlett had given him? Once when my brother Bob had gone under the water with cramps, a man pulled him from the river and rolled him over a barrel. Mom said that if Bob was allowed to breathe air again she would be the most grateful person in the world. And air had been given to Bob. Instead of Mom changing her mind and whipping him every step up the banks, why hadn't she gone to the church and thanked God for putting the air back in his body?

"Why is it, Mom?" I asked as these things came to mind, "that we don't ever go to the church to thank God?"

Mom bent over the tub of clothes and she did not answer.

On Sundays now, I began to sneak through the willow grove to the mouth of the Big Sandy. When I was even with the sandbar, I turned up the bank and hid behind a large maple tree and watched the people going into the red-brick church. As I watched them, I frowned. The people who walked inside the church wore clothes that had no patches and all of the boys had short hair, so short that you could see their ears from the distance of the maple trees.

I began to wonder if only those with patchless clothes and short hair were allowed to go inside the church. Maybe, I thought, the red-brick church is for those who own the good clothes, and maybe the rivers and the willows and the maples and the birch and the sycamore are for boys like me. Maybe this was the reason the family had never gone here. But, if this were true, I thought, God had surely cheated these people.

"You must be grateful for what you have," Mom had once said to me.

There was no boy in the valley that was more grateful for the rivers. And I sat along the banks thinking of how grateful I should be. If I wanted to thank God, I could thank Him right here. And my voice would carry over the tops of the willows like the smoke from the stack of a paddle wheel. It would pass over the town, higher and higher, above the top of the hills and be heard the same as the low chirp of the peewee bird.

iv

Winter had come to the riverbanks. The air was cool and sharp, and the rivers were beautiful. There were thin layers of ice along the edges of the rivers, and the leaves that had missed the current had been captured by the ice, and the meager sun shone and turned the leaves many colors. Now and then a brown ball would fall from a giant sycamore tree and break through the ice and the water would bubble out and run in small streams across the surface.

One day as I was sitting on the riverbank, I heard a group of boys coming through the willows. Christmas was only a few days off. At the church, the boys said, sacks of hard candy would be given to all the young people. Anyone who wants a sack could have it. All you had to do was to walk inside the church and get it.

As I watched the splinters of river ice, I thought only of the tall sacks of hard rock candy they had talked about. To them the candy might not have meant much, but to me it was something that cost more than I ever hoped to earn.

During the next few days, all I thought about was the sack of candy. I watched the rivers, silent now and with little current. I thought of walking inside the church and getting my sack of candy and as quickly as possible hurrying back inside the willow grove and working my way to the creek. Of course people inside the church would stare. But if I was fast on my feet, they wouldn't have long to stare.

As Christmas day came nearer, I began to sneak to the top of the bank and measure with my eyes the distance from the giant maple to the door of the church. And the more I measured the distance, the farther it seemed to be. While I was inside the church I would not have the time to stop after I had picked up my sack of candy to thank God for it. But then, I could do this easy enough when I reached the banks of the river again. Maybe, when I grew up and earned enough money to buy good clothes and have my hair cut, I could go back inside the church and thank Him proper.

Christmas day came at last to the valley. I was more scared than I had ever been in my life, more scared than the day the *Gordon C. Green* had slipped past me from the center of the Ohio.

I didn't bother to clean up before I left the house. I was afraid if I even washed my face that the rest of the family might know I was up to something. All I wanted was the tall sack of candy.

At the mouth of Catlettscreek, I stopped and bent over the small stream and splashed the cold water against my face, and the wind dried it and cold pimples ran up and down my back. As I thought of walking inside the church, the bumps grew larger than the wind could make them.

I hurried to the mouth of the Big Sandy and waited at the top of the bank behind the maple until I was sure that everyone was inside the church. I closed my eyes a moment and then ran out from behind the maple and didn't stop till I was at the door of the church. I stood for a minute to catch my breath and maneuvered around in front of the door as carefully as I would have moved around a snapper turtle.

The door opened with a squeak and I sneaked inside. At the far end of the room a woman stood beside a large wooden table. On top of the table were white sacks. The woman at the table called out the name of a class and a group of girls stood and walked single file down the aisle. As they passed the table, they were each handed a sack. Then another name was called, and a group of boys even smaller than myself passed by the table, reaching for the sacks of candy that seemed so big that they weighed the boys down.

As I stood at the front end of the room, I became more scared than ever. All I could see were the tall sacks of candy.

Right now I was too scared to move, yet I had come much too far to turn back. I scanned the room for the boys that I had seen at the river. I waited until they stood and started down the aisle, and then I fell in behind them like a duck that belongs to the same flock. I kept my eyes peeled to the floor, never once looking up. The legs of the table came into sight and I raised my head and stared into the eyes of the woman at the table.

"This boy is not in my class," she said, in a voice that seemed to shake the walls of the church.

"Nor mine either," another woman answered from the first bench.

"Nor mine," another voice said.

"He doesn't belong here at all."

Tears filled my eyes, and for a minute I was too scared to move. People were staring at me and many of them were shaking their heads. I knew now that all I wanted was to make it back to the rivers. This red brick church was not for me. I realized that I had been planning on getting something that did not belong to me. I turned and ran as fast as I could, down the steps of the church, and I didn't stop even at the small creek. I splashed in and the water circled my knees, and on the other side I fell to the sand and buried my head in my arms and cried. A short time ago, the sack of candy had meant almost as much to me as the two rivers. Now it meant nothing. Even if I had gotten it, I couldn't have taken it home. They would have thought that I had stolen it—or begged it, which would have been worse.

I stayed on the banks of the river below the house until the shadows crossed the water. Tears had frozen on my face and where I had waded the creek my legs were so cold they were numb. Then I heard footsteps on the frozen grass. And when I looked up Mom was standing over me. She did not quarrel because I had stayed away from home so long without her knowing where I was. She knelt beside me and I felt her arms around my shoulders.

"Hush now," she said. "Times come that even a man has to tell what's wrong. Tell me."

And stuttering worse than a jaybird I told her how I had wanted to steal the sack of candy, expecting her to break a willow switch at any moment.

But there were tears in her eyes too. And she held me close.

"Maybe it is better for our kind to give our thanks under the willows here. Prayers have far enough to climb without being hemmed in by the wall and the roof of an old building."

"But," I said, "maybe God don't know that I'm down here. He didn't see me in the church, and I didn't see Him."

"Hush now with foolish talk," Mom said. "If He can see a little bird like a sparrow, you know that He can see a big boy like you."

Mom pulled a handkerchief from her pocket and wet it over her tongue and wiped my face and the wind dried it.

And that evening Mom left the house and did not come back until after dark. I heard her come in during the night and pull the covers over us as she always did. But she stayed by our bed longer than usual this time. And the next morning when I woke I felt something hard under my pillow and when I reached down to find out what it was, I pulled out a small sack. And inside the sack was hard rock candy.

I jumped from the bed and ran into the room where Mom and Dad slept. "Look, Mom!" I yelled. "Look what God has given us!"

"'Pon my word," Mom said, "who'd have thought a prayer could have traveled that fast? Now, if you want to make the Lord happy, you'll share with the rest of the family."

As I walked out of the room, I wondered why my brothers and sisters didn't ask the Lord for a sack of candy themselves. I sneaked a handful out of the sack and stuck it into my pocket, so that they wouldn't know how much the Lord had given me. I divided the rest with them and then I ran to the riverbank to eat what was in my pocket.

When I reached the bank, I was so happy that I wanted to run and shout to both rivers. I looked into the clouds and thought of my prayer scaling the blue walls faster than a stream of smoke. But as I ran through the trees, I slipped over a stump and fell to the earth. The hard rock candy fell out of my pocket and rolled over the sand, picking up sand like a snowball scooping up snow. One by one the pieces rolled down the steep bank and into the river. The Lord had seen me sneak the candy into my pocket back at the house. Mom was right: He didn't have any trouble at all seeing me here on earth.

v

Miss Stigill was an important woman in town. She

could and would call the police if any of us boys even so much as stepped a toe on her lawn. When she called, the law came in a hurry. She was important. Funny, though, it is her dog that I remember much better than any important thing she did for the town.

The dog was a big bulldog, and since Miss Stigill was his owner he had the freedom of the town to romp as he pleased. He took advantage of it too. Almost every day the big bulldog used to come to the Leaning Tower and chase Mom's cats. Usually he didn't catch one, but if he did, he closed his powerful jaws and crushed it like an egg shell. My sisters would find the dead cat and hold a burial for it along the banks of the rivers. Crying, flowers, preaching, and all: a fitting tribute indeed for a plain old alley cat.

From our house, the big dog would usually meander over to where James, Bob, Jerry, Tom Harkness, and other river boys had set an old outdoor privy against a willow, to make a clubhouse for their private gang. Instead of gold, they stole corn, watermelons, muskmelons, and about anything else to eat that was not tied down. If it was tied down, it took them a little longer to untie it. The big bulldog would scratch around a few muskrat holes and then he would walk up to the clubhouse, hist his leg and wet down both the inside and outside of the clubhouse. Truth be known, he was about as unwanted around the clubhouse as me—him for histing and wetting down, and me for not being big enough to run if they were caught on a raid. Truth be known, too, there were many times that I felt like wetting down the clubhouse myself.

One day a special meeting was called by James, and the

gang planned a way of stopping the big bulldog. They began by trying to coax the animal to them. It failed from the very beginning. The big dog turned his head and walked away just as if he knew that because he belonged to Miss Stigill he was a little above associating with river trash.

"Maybe you ain't talking right to the dog," Riff Harder said to James. "Maybe you got to use society talk on him just like old Miss Stigill does. That dog is used to highfalutin' words."

"Come here, your highness," James said, snapping his fingers. The big dog turned and eyed James, wagged his stub-tail a little, and didn't budge.

"Nope," James said, "talking ain't the problem."

Riff Harder said, "Shucks, no wonder he didn't come to you. Your highness is the name for a girl dog."

"Do you think a plain dog is smart enough to know the difference?" James said.

"Well," Riff Harder said, rubbing his chin, "he's smart enough to know to hist his leg instead of squatting, ain't he?"

"Come on over here, mister highness," James said, snapping his fingers again and making a clicking noise with his mouth.

The stub-tail of the bulldog wagged harder now and he moseyed slowly over toward the clubhouse.

"Hand me the turpentined corn cob," James said. "Pet him on the head and I'll reach around the other end and finish off his histing days here at the clubhouse."

One poke and the eyes of the big bulldog set in the back of his head. His howl raised the sand along the riverbanks.

Everyone took for cover—some up the bank, some in the river, and I climbed the bent back of an old willow. Then the big dog got his bearings and shot up the riverbank like a stray bullet.

I don't know what happened to the beast from this point on. No doubt he reached home a sick dog. And no doubt Miss Stigill never found out his real problem. She was much too dignified to even suspect the dog's trouble would be under his tail.

CHAPTER 6

In the same year that my family moved into the Leaning Tower, the small house where I had been born was lifted by the strong currents of the two rivers and carried down the big Ohio. Dad was able to save but little of the furniture—just what he could haul on his back before the rivers swelled too high. Yet, Dad did not fret over furniture lost to the rivers. The rivers took away but they also gave.

During the seven years that we lived in the Leaning Tower, Dad had the opportunity to accumulate more furniture than he could have bought in a lifetime. He had piles of it stored in the big two-story house. And Mom was never a person to allow anything that could be mended to pass by—and she could mend anything. This furniture was called "drift furniture." It was the only kind we ever had in our house. And it filled many houses in Catlettsburg, including some of the better homes. Of course in these homes it was never referred to as drift furniture; it came from a relative far away, or it had been handed down by poor old Grandpa Whatshisname. "He did so want this piece of furniture to remain in the family."

There was one good thing about drift furniture: you could pull it from the rivers and no bill collector was attached. To me this was the greatest advantage of all. The bill collector had taken on the proportions of a Jesse James for our family. We had learned to spot bill collectors long before they reached our home and to spread the word that they were coming. As we dodged around the Leaning

Center Street during the 1937 flood, Catlettsburg.

"In the same year that my father moved into the Leaning Tower, the small house where I had been born was lifted by the strong currents of the two rivers and carried down the big Ohio."

Tower on our way to the riverbanks, they hollered at us, calling us all by our first names. It wouldn't have surprised me if one of them had opened his little black bag and pulled out a gun and shot Mom on the spot for a past bill. With the drift furniture you could be sure that the original owner would not come to claim it. Most of it had traveled a long way and, like the used clothing from Huntington, it would never be recognized in Catlettsburg.

We sat in the second story of the Leaning Tower and watched entire houses float down the Ohio. Sometimes only the roof would be sticking out of the muddy surface, and a man might be riding it like the back of a horse, waiting for the house to be washed ashore. If he secured the house to the bank he claimed it. Maybe he had been the original owner or maybe not. Sometimes men came down with a small joeboat attached to the house, pulling the oars through the currents and trying to land the house by eating distance inch by inch.

The expense of hauling a house back up river to its original location usually reached more than the actual value of the house. The man who rode it was known as a "drifter." He would stay with the house until it beached, when he would block it up and try to sell it. If he could not sell the house, he would remain with it until he became restless and then he would let the rivers take it and pass it farther down to another drifter.

The owners rode the houses down river too, either to claim them or to save the furniture inside. Sometimes the houses were stripped down and hauled back up the valley in wagons drawn by mules. After a flood, there were usually long lines of mule-drawn wagons coming into the valley with timber that held the markings of the rivers.

During a flood, paddle-wheel captains and their crews kept a sharp lookout for drift. Entire trees, roots and all, came speeding down the rivers, hitting each other and sailing high into the air like rockets and plunging back below the surface. They might drift just under the surface, unseen and likely to tear the bottom from a paddle wheel.

Boats chugged slowly up river blowing their whistles, signaling as far ahead as possible, because to turn for another boat to pass would require more distance, now that the flood made the current much stronger. They often chugged close to the bank, so close that they brushed the tops of submerged trees. The center of the big river held the current. And the great paddle wheels churned up the tops of the trees and threw them into the air with muddy sprays of water.

So close to the bank, the captain knew that there was more to watch for than snags and brush. Men who had landed buildings and large pieces of furniture hid at the edge of the water, and as the boats crawled past during the night they sneaked out with tow lines and fastened them to the big boats. The paddle wheel would go churning up river pulling the tow until the shadows left the rivers. When daylight came, the man would loose his tow, tie up to the bank, and wait for night and another paddle wheel.

Dead horses, cattle, dogs, sheep, goats, chickens, and every other type of animal or fowl came floating down the currents, bloated and bobbing out of the water. Often their carcasses hit snags and remained to rot. Sometimes the animals and fowls would be alive in the rivers, holding to anything that offered footing or headrest; and the buzzards came from the hills and circled them, waiting with the patience of time.

Horses, ponies, and mules came down the rivers with only their manes or tails trailing the surface and people along the shores would spot the hair and word would sweep over land that a human being had been spotted drifting with the currents. Most times it was only an animal, but humans were also pulled from the rivers, bloated and eaten by fish or buzzards. Seldom were their names known. Those who had been drowned in the floods might never be found, and people gathered along the banks and held services, and threw flowers into the rivers to float over their watery graves.

Outdoor privies outnumbered all buildings that floated down the swollen rivers. They came in all sizes, all shapes, all colors. Now they drifted through the streets of town, hugging the buildings and lodging wherever they could dodge the currents. People with indoor privies cursed the outdoor ones for lodging along the streets of town. The Younger Women's Society stood by heroically to see that the outdoor privies were dislodged, so that the river would carry the unsightly buildings elsewhere. Since the rivers had crept up the banks like a thief and stolen ours, we watched for replacements.

Dad had a kind of "green thumb" when it came to catching a privy for planting where our old one had stood. He always managed to take a better one than we had lost. One year he even caught a five-seater. In my lifetime, I never saw the equal in Catlettsburg or surrounding areas.

Second Ward School (in background).
Photo courtesy of Billy C. Clark.

"When the rivers settled over the town for a long period, we
gathered what we could carry and crossed the town to the
schoolhouse that stood on high land on the foot of the hills."
(Author's note: The schoolhouse, the largest and most costly
in the valley was completed in 1892, served as both high
school and grade school. I attended the school for eight
years.)

ii

We had not been able to ride out all the floods in the
Leaning Tower. When the rivers settled over the town for a
long period, we gathered what we could carry and crossed
the town to the small schoolhouse that stood on high land

at the foot of the hills. I liked to stay in the schoolhouse during high water; the rivers could never rise high enough for me. There were lots of boys my age to play with—boys with hair as long as mine. And there was more to eat here than at home. Three meals a day. Imagine!

People slept in every room of the schoolhouse. Long lines of small cots were placed wherever space allowed, so close together that you could wiggle your toe and be in the bed of your neighbor.

I waited at night for Mom and Dad to go to sleep. Then I sneaked out of bed and joined other boys in chalk and eraser fights. When morning came, it looked as if a chicken had stepped in a white bucket of paint and walked up and down the blackboards. And we carved on the desks, leaving enough shavings and sawdust to hold a square dance in the room.

My brothers and sisters hated staying at the schoolhouse during high water. The larger girls were all kept together, and each night their names were called and they were bed-checked. All the older boys hung around outside the girls' rooms, climbing to the window sills, and peeping and whistling, sneaking them out and wandering the hills. There was so much noise around and inside the schoolhouse that they were seldom heard. Babies cried all night and women fed them from the breast.

The Younger Women's Society took command of the situation here at the schoolhouse. They fed us food sent up by the state, and corraled us like cattle. When they were not fighting us, they fought among themselves. Trouble was brewing among some of the women of the town. Earlier there had been just a plain Women's Society. Then a few women got together and formed the Younger Women's Society. Soon after that, the older ones dissolved like carbide in a miner's lamp, while the Younger Women's Society increased its membership. Some of the members were so old that they hobbled on canes, with faces so wrinkled I couldn't imagine how they could squint past and see daylight. Powder would fill and hide the wrinkles, they thought, and they shoveled it on like coal in the furnace of a paddle wheel. They had all "grayed early" and some of them could barely totter. Only the government, when pension time rolled around, knew their ages.

One of these women was the mother [she could easily have been the grandmother] of a girl that had caught my brother James's eye at school. You should have seen him! At mealtime when we all gathered in the long lines fighting to reach the soup pots, James stuck his head from the back of the line to see which member of the Society would be serving. If it happened to be the mother of the girl he was stuck on, he would try to bribe me to go through the line a second time for him.

"Look as sad as you can," he would say, squinting toward the soup pots. "Act just like it was your first time through. You ought to be able to sneak through again." What he didn't know was that I was trying to sneak through for the third time myself. My stomach was already bloated as a catfish in a crawdad bed.

When this particular woman saw James during the day, he took on airs, acting as if he were part of the rescue force, directing the boats to the banks with their supplies.

Or, if he was indoors, he acted as if he were helping to rearrange the cots to make more room. You would have thought James was in charge of the whole operation. If he could have convinced anyone and made his way to serving the soup he would have had it made.

Each time we went to the schoolhouse, Mom swore the Leaning Tower would not be there when we returned. Each time it was—leaning a little more, but still there. And we all pitched in to scrape mud from it and give the mud back to the rivers.

And then came 1936. "I think I'll look for another house," Dad said. "If I wait until the rivers are high, I won't be able to rent a chicken coop on high ground. I don't believe the house is safe any longer. The ground is loose underneath, and it won't stand another flood."

Overview of Catlettsburg during the 1937 flood.

"...and it won't stand another flood." (Author's note: It didn't. The Leaning Tower was washed away by the 1937 flood, one of the greatest floods in the history of the valley.)

CHAPTER 7

The house that Dad rented was much smaller than the Leaning Tower. It stood on high ground at the other side of town, using the hills for a back rest. It was close enough to the grade school to hoist a rock through a window if you could curve it around the trees. Tall black oaks leaned over the side of the hills and touched the roof. At night, when the wind was blowing, limbs swished against the roof with a noise that could put you to sleep. Catlettscreek wormed its way toward the two rivers, so close to the small house that the hum of the water could be heard from the porch.

Dad figured that the smaller house was an even better bargain than the Leaning Tower. It was surely run down, but Dad's hands could make it livable. One side of the house was on stilts and under this high side of the house the people before us had kept chickens. Dad planned to convert the space into a workshop where he could mend shoes at night.

The back yard had, at one time, been a hog lot. Old hog tracks marked all the floors of the rooms in the house, indicating that the animals had been made to feel a part of the family before us. Mom had no intentions of raising hogs, so she figured to turn the ground for garden. The ground would be well fertilized. In fact, on nights when the wind swept over the yard and into the windows, Dad said the wind had been so enriched by the hog remains that you could have pushed a hole in it and stuck in a seed, and it would have sprouted.

Moving had been the hardest part of the exchange. We had nothing but our sweat and our backs. The big carried the big and the small carried the small—with me getting cheated all the way, I believed. The luckier ones carried chairs. When we stopped along the way, they had something to sit in and brace their tired backs. In a long line resembling the gypsy caravans that came each year to the valley, we crossed the streets of town with our plunder, stopped to rest where we would not tie up traffic, then picked up and walked on.

How happy Mom was with this house! She had become the proud owner of an indoor privy—white commode, wash basin with mirror, and all the trimmings! Mom cautioned us about flushing the commode more than was necessary. Anything that might increase household bills was important to us. A pull on the brass handle brought swirling water into the bowl, churning like the whirlpool beyond the snag at the mouth of Catlettscreek.

The year before we moved from the Leaning Tower, the worst of all things that could happen in an outdoor privy occurred: a writing spider came one day to spin his web. He latched one end onto a horseweed stalk growing behind the privy, and the other onto a corner post.

A writing spider is a large yellow-and-black spider that spins a web as large as a wash tub. Here in the valley, it is said by the old people that this spider has strange powers: when he hears your name, he writes it in his web and takes your life before the evening sun goes down. What if he hears it at night? I suppose in this case you live until the next sun goes down. Sure enough, inside his web are to be

Writing Spider.
Photo courtesy of Billy C. Clark.

"Here in the valley, it is said by the old people that this spider had strange powers: when he hears your name, he writes it in his web and takes your life before the evening sun goes down."

seen thick white zigzags that resemble letters of the alphabet.

Our big writing spider quickly filled his web with fat flies. It seemed reasonable to believe, after hearing of his powers from Mom, that each of the flies had a name and the spider had heard them in fly talk and written them in the web.

In the morning the early sun glistened on his web and the small beads of dew rolled along the silver fibers and dripped-dripped on the long green leaves of the horse-weed. There sat the spider as independent as a spider can get, ready to write the first name he heard. When I walked to the privy, I kept my eyes cocked.

James used to catch me inside the privy and say, "Who's in there?"

"You know who I am!" I would answer, cold chills creeping over me, even though it was the hot summertime.

"Nope," he'd say, waiting a minute. "Don't believe I recognize your voice at all. Who did you say you were?"

"I'm your brother!" I would answer, making ready to set a speed record from the privy to the house.

"My brother? Which one?"

I would think for a minute. "The littlest one."

"Well, then," he would say in a slow drawl, "you must be..."

And out of the privy I would come just as fast as my legs could take me.

ii

Jerry had established himself a business to be envied—enviable not so much for the work as for the money he made. But moving from the Leaning Tower ruined it.

Jerry was not yet twelve years old, broad-shouldered, with powerful arms and legs. Much as a boy might develop himself a paper route around a neighborhood, Jerry had developed a slop route. He began by gathering old buckets from the dumps along the banks of the two rivers. Taking the buckets around to our neighbors, he propositioned to haul away their slop, free. Then he traveled to the outskirts of Catlettsburg and made arrangements to sell all the slop he could gather to a hog-raiser, a big curly-headed man named Joe Mueller who had better than a hundred hogs and, according to Jerry, little'ns coming all the time.

Jerry left the house before daylight. Searching neighbor's slop cans like a stray dog, he filled his buckets one at a time and left them back of the Leaning Tower until he could come home from school and take them across town to the hog man. But a short time after his business had got its start, he was forced to find another storage place. When the winds came from the rivers, it brought the smell of slop so strong that you could hardly bear it inside the house. So he had to store his slop a little farther down the bank.

Within a year, Jerry had made himself a pushcart. He traded the junk dealer some iron for four roller-skate wheels and he made a wagon from driftwood he gathered along the rivers. Then he expanded his route. He left earlier in the morning. But still his route was too long to cover before school began. So he finished half in the morning and half when school was out in the evening, reaching the hog man long after darkness was in the valley. Here, under lights, he waited for his slop to be graded.

There were many different grades of slop. A good price was paid for potato peelings, vegetables, bread, and other soft foods that could be easily digested by hogs. But, according to the hog man, first-grade slop had—just like every thing else, he reckoned—gone to pot. In other words, good slop was hard to find. Few people knew anything about slop. Have it their way and they'd feed a hog anything. A man with common sense should know that a hog can't eat paper, tin cans, rags, and such. He'd beckon to Jerry to come closer, using a finger that Jerry claimed to resemble a boar hog's tooth, and say: "Trouble with this whole damn world is that no one knows what to feed hogs. They're as useless when it comes to sloppin' hogs as a trimmed jack." And so Jerry's slop was poured into a long trough where Jerry would wade through it, taking out any impurities. He would stop at Catlettscreek each evening and wash the slop off his legs and arms in the waters of the creek.

And then one day at the junk dealer's Jerry spotted a set of balloon-tired wheels. He spent almost a month's money to buy them. But it paid off, because he built a bigger cart and hauled twice as much slop as before.

You should have seen him! In the summer he would push the big cart around the neighborhood with six or eight buckets of slop on it, and the flies would be swirling around him in black clouds. In the winter the snow and ice would glisten from it and the steam would rise from the warm buckets of slop like pots cooking on top of a hot stove.

The slop business was looking up and it might have remained that way if Jerry hadn't kept stopping at Curt

Parsons' service station.

The right tire on Jerry's cart had developed a slow leak, and every day he'd stop at the gas station to air up. Now the air hose was next to the gasoline pump, and a man stopping for air was also blocking cars from the pump. Squinting his eyes at the sign above the air hose, making sure that it still said FREE AIR, Jerry would stretch the hose down to his tire. Cars pulled in and waited behind him, testing the stench that trailed back to them from the cart, rolling up their windows, and cursing Jerry for all they were worth. But if they thought they could cause him to hurry and take a chance of blowing his tire, they had another few good whiffs of slop coming. Jerry would not be pushed.

To run him off did little good. Curt Parsons couldn't be at his station every minute of the day. And as soon as his back was turned, Jerry was loading up. So Curt Parsons finally came to the Leaning Tower.

That night Jerry lay in bed and cried, rubbing his calloused hands over his eyes and the welts on his body. He said to me, "I've took my last whipping!"

It hurt me to see Jerry cry. I was far closer to him than any of the family. I could not forget the many evenings that he had stopped at a small grocery store on his way home from the hog man's place and bought bread. We had gone to the banks of the rivers and there after dark had sat down and crunched up a loaf of bread and maybe a cake or two, if business was good. We had been raised on bread and water gravy. I cannot remember eating an egg during all the time I lived at the Leaning Tower.

Whippings were all-important at home, and all too

many as far as I was concerned. A woman would come to the Leaning Tower, usually someone important in town, and accuse us boys of tramping through her yard on our way home from school. Maybe we had sneaked into her yard and tore down the limbs of an apple tree.

"I could have called the police," the woman would say to Mom. "I could force you to pay for the damage your boys have done. But I don't want to make things any harder for you than you have it now. However, I must insist on seeing them punished."

And while this woman watched we were stripped and whipped—hard. Like the time I walked past Miss Stigill's house and the bulldog came out at me. I hit him in the side of the head with a rock.

"Come right up on my porch, that brat did," she said to Mom, hardly taking time out to breathe. "Caught my little dog asleep and tried to kill him. That boy bears watching!"

"We've enough troubles to worry about," Mom would say later, after the whippings. "What would we do if they called the police? They might try to take one of our boys from us and send him to reform school. Better to give the whippings. It's all part of being poor."

After we moved from the Leaning Tower, Jerry had to leave the slop business. A railroad split the town in half, and Jerry couldn't cross it with the pushcart. He had to take his cart almost a mile down river to a small underpass. Jerry traveled at a snail's pace, and when he went through the underpass he tied up traffic about as far as the eye could see—the slop steaming, the horns honking, and Jerry with all the time in the world. Then, too, our neighbors here along the hills had their own hogs to feed.

Boyd County Courthouse, Catlettsburg.
Photo courtesy of the <u>Daily Independent</u>, Ashland, Kentucky.

"There was a reason for Mom choosing me out of the entire family to appear in court with her."

CHAPTER 8

Mom and Dad had spent many hours of labor trying to keep the Leaning Tower in shape. And after all that work it still became too treacherous for us, poor as we were.

Less than two months after we left the Leaning Tower, we were served a summons to appear in court. Brice Flanners claimed that Dad owed back rent. What had really happened was obvious: now that Dad had moved, there was little chance Brice Flanners would ever be able to rent the Leaning Tower without major repairs, and the old house wasn't worth repairing.

What proof did Dad have that he owed Brice Flanners nothing? Only his word! But wasn't this a world of who you were and who you knew, rather than how honest you were? "What will you do, Mason?" Mom asked, wringing her hands.

"What can I do? I'll have to pay, I suppose," Dad said.

"Pay for what!" Mom screamed. "You owe nothing! Brice Flanners is the one that should be taken to court and tried. And anyway, how will you pay?"

Dad lowered his head. "The same way I've always paid in this world: with sweat and blood."

"Your pa stood by and watched while his land was taken from him!" Mom said furiously.

"Pa was an honest man," said Dad. "Died honest. How many others here in the valley can claim that?"

"Will honesty buy bread for the children?" Mom answered. "Maybe Brice Flanners' lying will come home to him someday. But we'll starve while we wait."

"We'll make out somehow," Dad said. "We always have."

Mom stomped her feet on the floor.

"Maybe you will!" she said. "But I'm tired of it. All my life I have lived humbling here in this valley—" tears came from her eyes—"and I've took a lot from people just because I was poor and made to feel that way. But right here and now I've took for the last time! I'll never be pushed around again!"

"Now, don't you worry, Bert," Dad said. "It is not you who's being pushed. I'll find a way."

"Don't stand there and take sides with that crook!" Mom said. "Not here in front of the children! If the children go hungry because of him it's me who's being pushed. If it's a court fight he wants, I'll fight him."

Dad stood silent now and did not speak again.

In the days that followed, it was Mom who took the piece of paper that held the summons and read it to us again and again. She gathered us all around her in a little group and read each word slowly. And as she stuttered over the larger words she stopped and looked at us, and tears rolled down her face. "I might have to leave you and go to jail for a while," she would say, "but I won't let Brice Flanners mistreat you."

And we all puckered our mouths and cried with her.

"Your daddy might stand by and see him take bread from our table, but not me," Mom would add. And she would talk of how Brice Flanners had been robbing people here in the valley for many years. He had bought up many old buildings and rented them to the poor. Most would not have been considered good chicken houses. Time and time again the old buildings were condemned by the state. Then Brice Flanners usually bought a few gallons of cheap paint and a fifth of wine, got a wino from Bloody Front to paint in exchange for the wine, and passed the next inspection.

The day came for Mom to appear in court. James, Bob, Jerry, and my two older sisters went off to school, my two younger sisters were left with our closest neighbor, and I went with Mom. There was a reason for Mom choosing me out of the entire family to appear in court with her. I was the only boy she had left with hair reaching to my shoulders. She would rely on the sympathy I might get in court.

Just inside the courtroom, it dawned on me that I might be headed for jail and I began to cry. Mom patted me on the head, seeming to be pleased that I was crying, and walked into the room like the presiding judge.

The court had not yet been opened, but the short, gray-headed judge was there. He walked quickly up the aisle to meet Mom, he looked back over the crowded room, and motioned for Brice Flanners to come.

"How are you today, Mrs. Clark?" he asked. The judge knew Mom. She had done house cleaning and washing for him.

"I'm feeling poorly," Mom answered, her mouth quivering.

"I want the chance to talk to both you and Mr. Flanners," the judge said. "We have many cases on the docket and I believe there is no need for adding yours. I think we can square your case up with a little talk. Perhaps some settlement."

"I've given them long enough to pay!" Brice Flanners said.

"We don't owe you!" Mom said, her face turning red and her chest heaving.

"Prove it to the court then!" said Brice Flanners. He threw out his bony little chest. The crows was watching and he was putting on a show. "And now besides the rent," he said, "I ought to make you pay for the damages them river tramps of yours have done to..."

Whamm! Mom landed a blow that shook Brice Flanners' glasses to the end of his weasel nose. He wavered and fell against the side of a court bench.

"Stop, stop, Mrs. Clark!" the judge said.

But it was too late. People had risen from their seats and pushed the judge out of reach. And Brice Flanners did not hold equal terms as far as the people were concerned. Many of the crowd were even poorer than us.

Mom shuffled around Brice Flanners like a game chicken, waiting for him to stand up again. When he reached his feet he headed for the courtroom door. Mom was close behind him, and I was behind Mom. He crossed the courthouse yard toward the Chesapeake and Ohio railway track. Mom gained. And seeing that he couldn't outrun her, he stopped at the edge of the tracks to bargain.

"Now, Mrs. Clark, I'm sorry. Now, Mrs. Clark!"

Mom came on like a charging bull and Brice Flanners turned again to run. I was close to Mom and I could hear her puff like a malley engine. She bent over and picked up a railroad rock, and sailed it after Brice Flanners. If it had been shot from a gun it could have gone no truer. Smack! I saw

Brice Flanners' glasses fall and he sprawled after them. Mom stood over him. She hit him again and again. People gathered to try to pull her loose. Then I made a dash for Brice Flanners and swung at him with all my might. I missed him and hit a crosstie. The skin came off my knuckles and the blood oozed out.

A siren blew and the police car pulled up near the tracks. A policeman led Mom off, with me trailing behind,

Pike's Crossing, Catlettsburg.

"She bent over and picked up a railroad rock, and sailed it after Brice Flanners. If it had been shot from a gun it could have gone no truer."

crying because I was sure we were headed for jail. Mom wept and mumbled, "I've always tried to live decent. People wouldn't let me."

The policeman drove us to the City Building and took us into a small office to wait. Here we sat, both crying.

After a while the door opened and Dad walked in. "Let's go home, Bert," he said, patting her on the arm. "Everything's going to be all right."

That night, I told my brothers and sisters how I'd fought Brice Flanners a terrible fight. How I'd stood up to him and popped him in the jaw hard enough to turn him a flip-flop. I stuck out my fist that had connected with the crosstie and swung it hard into thin air to show the force of the blow.

Just wait, I thought as I lay in bed that night. The next person that laughs at my hair or clothes is really in for it. I'll hunker no more. I felt my knuckles. I had told the tale so many times I almost believed it was true myself.

The wind sung through the trees, the moon lit up the room somewhat, and the wind played with the tips of the oaks. Mom had been fined one dollar for contempt of court, and the case had been thrown out. We had beat Brice Flanners. We were free of the Leaning Tower.

CHAPTER 9

We were no strangers to the hills, least of all Mom. Often when she was in a happy mood she would laugh and tell us how Grandpa Hewlett said he was born so far up the Big Sandy Valley that he'd been able to straddle the river to wash his face. Mom, herself, was born deep in the hills twelve miles up the valley at a toe hold on the hills known as Buchanan, Kentucky. Three miles walk out of the hollow and she could stand on a knoll and stare at the small single-tracked railroad. The train crawled down the valley like a caterpillar worm with its joints loose, smoke puffing from the big malley engine and trailing off over the river. The railroad was the only means of transportation in and out of the valley. The Big Sandy River had been left to pool; it was so shallow in places that you could wade across it.

When she was sixteen, Mom had taken her first ride on the train. This had been a great day. More dreaming had gone into this day than she could tell, and her eyes lighted up even now as she talked of it. Before boarding the train, she needed some sort of luggage to take with her. The fact that she was traveling only twelve miles down river to Catlettsburg didn't matter. Everyone that boarded the train carried luggage. With luggage, there was a feeling of going somewhere. People gathered at the small cow-path station, elected one of their number to flag down the train, and waited hours for it to crawl down the valley. The men wore big handle-bar mustaches, and the women wore their

Passenger train near Catlettsburg during high water.

"When she was sixteen Mom had taken her first ride on the train."

Sunday clothes. They carried "trading goods" in feed sacks stitched with designs that showed long hours of needlework under oil lamps. Mom's mother had pieced her bag out of a flowered feed sack. There were few bags like this in the valley, and Mom felt proud to hold it. She stood at the station, listening to the people talk.

"How far down you travelin' today, John?"

"All the way. Five miles below Catlettsburg. Clear to Ashland where the train's made up."

"Lordy! You've a long way to go."

"Yes sir, a long stretch o' rail. Wouldn't want to make the trip every day."

Kin gathered to say good-by. They hugged the necks of the people that boarded the train, then crossed over the tracks and ran along the side of the hill to wave until the train was out of sight. Inside, folks strained their heads out of the open windows to wave back and then drew back in the seats to sweat out the bumpy ride. Men chewed tobacco and spat on the floor when the conductor wasn't looking. After they got tired of the trip, they spat on the floors even with the conductor looking. Coal dust drifted through the train as if it were being piped inside, and just when the big engine built up steam it had to stop. Someone had flagged her down, or, maybe a cow had crossed the track halfway and lowered her head to bellow louder than the big malley engine. The owner of the cow hurried over a knoll, waving his fist just daring the engineer not to stop. After all, cows had been in the valley long before the trains.

The valley's bony ridges stand high. Many of them are shaped like the point of a layoff plow. From a distance, they gouge into white clouds, and seem to be harrowing them like long white bottoms. From the top of the ridge just above the small house under the oaks, you could stand and look out over many miles of the valley. Mornings before the sun was up, a layer of fog as blue as a robin's egg quilted the lowlands. The wind swept from the ridges and thinned the fog, and the Big Sandy River, far below, looked narrow enough to step across; the Ohio could be crossed with a jump. The paddle-wheel boats looked the size of an acorn and the smoke from the stacker like the dying puff from a country match.

Traveling to the top of the ridges meant fighting through short-butted white oaks and untangling your feet from saw briers. I can tell you something about saw briers. Those small thorny vines would unthread a pair of pants as slick as you could do it with a sewing needle.

According to Mom these hills were the home of spirits and omens, both to be feared like a copperhead snake.

Late at evening, Mom would gather us all up and take us around the rim of the hills to an old deserted coal mine. As we walked, the beams of moonlight sifted through the black branches and streaked the path like rungs of a ladder, and all eight of us walked cautiously, trying to step on the beam rungs, pretending that to miss one was to fall off the top of the mountain. I remained as close to Mom as the other seven would allow me to get. The wind made a mournful sound through the tops of the trees. It always did whenever we were on our way to see spirits.

In a place where the hill dipped as sharp as a broken stick, the mine had been gouged deep into the earth.

*Martha, Kentucky Woodland, located just up the Big Sandy
River from Catlettsburg.*
Photo courtesy of Billy C. Clark.

*"According to Mom these hills were the home of spirits and
omens, both to be feared like copperhead snakes."*

Honeysuckle and wild opossom-grape vines crawled over its mouth like long flocks of hair, and the wind brushed the vines together and the sound echoed from the hole in the earth. No more than thirty feet from the mouth a giant weeping willow grew, branches hovering low to the earth, sweeping at the tips of grass beneath them. Here we huddled to wait for the spirit that dwelled inside the mine. Whenever the wind came up strong and the noise became louder, Mom cocked her ear and said, "Listen!"

And we would all scoot closer to her, afraid to look but unable to keep from looking, because we all wanted to see what a spirit looked like. As if things were not already bad enough, an owl wavered his lonesome voice from deep in the hollow and goose pimples crept all over me.

"Now's the time!" Mom would whisper. The girls' voices broke first. Mine followed. "Hush!" Mom scolded. "Don't cry! The spirit will hear us and not come out!"

This mouth was full of mine water like many deserted coal mines here in the hills. I wondered if the spirit would come swimming out with overhand strokes like my three brothers or dog-paddling like me.

Then some noise would come from the hills nearby. We all knew it was surely the spirit. "Lord help us!" cried Mom. As far as we were all concerned, it was far too late for help of any kind, and we screamed at the tops of our voices.

"You little dickenses!" Mom would say. "Now the spirit is gone. You've scared him away. I'll never bring you again!"

And back around the hill we went, as close to Mom as a cocoon is to the side of a tree. And Mom would talk along the way; she had seen the spirit. We were all quick to agree that we had seen it too. Once away from the mine, we became a little braver—but not too brave to keep from looking back over our shoulders. We wanted a head start in case the spirit followed.

Dad would be working late in the basement, mending shoes. "See anything?" he'd ask as Mom came in, a big grin on his face. "I wouldn't make fun, Mason!" Mom said. "Mockery is a bad omen!" And Dad would often say, "Well, I don't see why you have to go traipsing around the hills with the children to see a spirit. You could see one just as easy right here in your own back yard."

The tales of spirits and omens that Mom knew could raise the hair on your head. It did mine, and I had a lot of it to raise. To be by a window during a storm was a bad omen because glass drew lightning. Cats drew lightning worse than glass. Even the birds that gathered under the eaves at night carried an omen: if one ever made it into the room, a member of the family would die.

The wail of the owl was mournful enough from deep in the hollow. But it was worse yet if he came out of the hollow to hoot. Inside the house nearest his voice, there would be a death.

If the weather was too bad for traveling to the mine or other places in the hills where the spirits dwelled, Mom brought the supernatural right into the house. One of her favorites was to gather us all around a small table and have us place our open palms flat on top of it. In the dark, Mom would speak to the spirit, "If you hear me, spirit, and you are in the room, move the table!" If the table moved, which it usually did, whimpers came from around it. The whimpers came from eight frightened spirits.

When Dad came up from the basement, he'd feel his way into the room and say, "Careful, Bert, don't shove the table over and hurt one of the children."

"'Pon my word!" Mom would say, "you are bound and compelled to bring a bad omen to this house!"

I did not mind the spirits and omens much during the daytime. I walked around the hills daring them to come out into the open. I swelled out my chest, knocked the top from a daisy with my fist and shouted, "Come out, spirit! Come out, omen! Come out, you cowards! Come out and meet the fist that felled Brice Flanners!" But when darkness came, I would say to myself, "You must be crazy to have said a thing like that." I apologized a thousand times and, brother, that's a-plenty for a boy in the lower grades of school.

ii

If you mentioned fortunetellers to Mom she would denounce them with one breath and ask their location with the next. Like many of the older people of the valley, Mom believed that to know the future was to claim the power of God. Therefore, to tell fortunes was to join forces with the devil. It was an evil practice. But Mom had visited every fortuneteller she had ever heard about. She swore by the fortunetellers one minute and cursed them the next.

I have seen my mother scrub clothes until her knuckles bled to earn a dollar, buy fifty cents' worth of food for the family—usually a small sack of flour and neck bones—

borrow salt and seasoning from a neighbor, and save fifty cents for the fortuneteller. Some of them told your fortune by reading the lines in your palm and others with a deck of playing cards. The only difference I saw between the two was that the one using cards had a little more invested, because of the cost of the deck.

"First of all, Mrs. Clark," the fortuneteller would say to Mom, "you must tempt the spirits with a fifty-cent piece. Grease my palm with it and I'll see that the spirit is compensated. Spirits need a little coaxing."

Into her hands would go Mom's hard-earned fifty cents. Then the fortuneteller would stare at her as if she were probing the mind of a total stranger, even though she had known all about Mom for the past twenty years. She would rattle on, telling Mom things that even the youngest member of our family knew. This lasted for about fifteen minutes. And as sure as the sun would set beyond the hills, the fortuneteller would place her hand on her forehead as if she had been kicked by a mule. "Oh!" she would cry. "I feel the spirit going from me! I don't believe I can hold him long enough to finish the most important part of your fortune, Mrs. Clark! Oh! Oh! not even the last sentence! A veil is coming over the words!" She would reach into the air as if she were trying to snatch a fly. "Quickly, quickly! Mrs. Clark, grease my palm with another fifty cents before the spirit leaves us completely!"

"Oh, Lord!" Mom would say, "I don't have it." She looked around as if she expected to see a fifty-cent piece go floating past. "Do ... do you reckon, Mrs. Sharkey, that the spirit would credit me till Friday?"

Mrs. Sharkey would tilt her head slightly, roll her eyes, and say, "Mrs. Clark! You'll shame the spirit asking for credit. Let's hope it never heard you!"

Mom would say on the way home, "She's an evil woman akin to the devil. Never told me a damn thing I didn't already know!"

But we knew what Mom was really thinking. She was thinking what might have been told if she'd had the extra fifty cents.

iii

Above the house, along the first flat of the hill, stood a walnut grove. When the autumn frost came to the valley, the cold winds shook down most of the walnuts, and Jerry and I skinned out the limbs and knocked the rest down. You couldn't shake a walnut tree until the first frost had brittled the stems.

We gathered the walnuts into a heap and trampled them, breaking loose the hull from the shell. Then we beat them with rocks until our hands were blistered and browned from the stain, and dragged them down the rugged slope and spread them out on the roof so the wind and sun would dry them. The stain had to be dried from the walnuts before we could sell them. This took time, and we sat for days under the oaks in the back yard watching the bluejays sneak from the trees and steal walnuts one at a time.

It takes a lot of climbing, shaking, gathering, and hulling to fill a feed sack full of walnuts. We sold them to Elf

Gibbons, a merchant who lived a good mile from where we had gathered the walnuts. Elf Gibbons had two large walnut trees in his own back yard. I couldn't understand why he would pay us a dollar for the feed sack of walnuts when he had twice as many right at hand. All they needed was hulling out.

I asked Mom, "Why doesn't Elf Gibbons gather the walnuts in his own back yard? The wind has shaken them down, and he won't even have to skin his shins on the bark of the trees."

"He's afraid that he'll get the walnut stain on his hands," Mom said.

"The stain won't hurt him," I said.

"Society people don't go around with walnut stain on their hands," Mom said. "People might think he was too poor to buy walnuts. They'd be apt to laugh at him."

I looked at my hands, speckled with the heavy stain. I tried to decide if the part of the dollar I had earned was worth giving people another reason to laugh at me.

"But who'd want to be society?" Mom said. "The Lord put the walnut on the tree for people to gather and eat. If He'd thought for a minute that the stain would hurt them, He wouldn't have put it inside the hull."

Jerry and I took our money and traveled to the nearest store. We each bought popsicles. Popsicles now had a special bargain. On one popsicle stick somewhere among the great stack of popsicles at the store would be the word FREE. If you found this word on one of the sticks in your popsicle, you got another one free.

We walked back home on opposite sides of the road.

Jerry had bought a chocolate popsicle. To save me, I could not tell where the popsicle ended and his hands began, the stain was that heavy. I held the back of my hand toward him. The stain hadn't touched the backs. I shook the whiteness at him and said, "I'm society. You better keep to your side of the road."

"Shucks," Jerry answered, making a face, "I'm just a plain Clark boy."

I stuck my nose high into the air like old Miss Stigill, twisting toward his side of the road. Jerry was eating high on his popsicle and I wanted to squint along his stick to see if he had gotten a free stick. He didn't and neither did I. Just our luck.

iv

In the hills, we gathered herb roots—ginseng, yellow root, sweet anise, and sassafras. We found teaberry leaves, wild peppermint, cherry bark, and many others that we could sell or use for home remedies. Under the trees we went and the birds would be flying along the limbs watching us. A bluejay would scream from high in the trees, going from one to the other as if we'd set fire to the tree that he had left. We took pointed sticks to dig out the roots and knives to slit the bark.

Under the needle pine, I gathered mushrooms. When I first gathered them I expected to make a great heap of money. According to Mom, mushrooms were considered highfalutin' food by society. They may have been, but I never had much luck selling them in town. People seemed to be afraid that I had gathered toadstools instead of mushrooms. Underneath the stool the mushroom was pink and the toadstool was white. I used to sit for hours trying to think how I could add pink to white without getting caught, since there were many many times more toadstools than mushrooms. I gave up the whole idea after a while and took home what I gathered, and we ate them all, white or pink.

We saved most of the herbs. Once a year, Ben Puckett came along the foothills to buy them. He was an old man with hair as gray as old cotton, which came to a peak on the top of his head as well as on the end of his great, long beard. Up the road he would come, driving an old wooden wagon with an enormous gray-slated horse that he called Big By George. If the hair on a horse grayed with age as it did on humans, this horse must have been a thousand years old.

In the last years that Ben came, I had a dog. I had found him one day along the banks of Catlettscreek. At this time there were stray dogs all over the place. They roamed the hills and the streets of town, with bitches having their litters wherever they happened to be standing when the pups dropped. If they happened to be standing deep in society when the pups came, that was not the fault of the dog, but of nature. People gathered up the pups and threw them into the creek or the river.

Long ears or other hound marks gave pups a slim chance of escaping the water. Such hound-marked dogs might be sold. If the buyer believed the pup was from seasoned stock, that was his own fault. Chances were that the pup's only seasoning was from the weather he had been

147

Young Billy C. Clark's hound dog and hunting campanion, Lucy.
Photo courtesy of Billy C. Clark.

"In a country like mine, a hound dog was highly valued."

exposed to before someone found him. In a country like mine, a hound dog was highly valued, sometimes even higher than a man's wife, and often rightly so.

I had heard the whine of the small pup as I passed him along the creek. He was in a burlap sack with five other pups, all dead. I lifted him up and water poured from his mouth and rear. He was too young to have his eyes open.

If I took home a dog, I'd be in trouble with Mom for sure. And if any of this pup's ancestors had a streak of hound blood, the dog would have had to belong to

Methuselah, with no crossings since—he looked that unhoundlike. And he was bobtailed to boot.

I placed the small pup higher on the bank and walked off. I knew full well that I was too far up creek to actually hear the whine of the pup, and yet I could hear him as surely as I could see the bottom of the creek. Circumstances gave me and this pup a great many things in common. One day he would be laughed at because of his stub-tail and because he wasn't a hound. He was hungry. I was, too. In fact, I had come here to gather elderberries that I hoped to sell for making wine or jelly.

When I left the creek I carried the pup with me. I made a bed out of old rags and hid him under the floor of the house. Mom heard him whimper and thought something was after the chickens. She spotted him. "When morning comes," she said, "you'll march him right back to the creek where you found him!"

I lay in bed thinking now of the small pup that Mom thought was still under the house but that I knew was in the kitchen where I had sneaked him less than a hour ago. To take the pup back to the creek meant killing him. I couldn't do it. When morning came, I would take him somewhere. I didn't know where.

I was up early, but Mom already stood in the doorway of the kitchen. She had her hands on her hips as if she were thinking: wait until that boy comes downstairs!

"'Pon my word," she said, shaking her head and looking toward the corner where I had laid the pup the night before.

And there, in the corner, was Mom's big cat, Kitty

Mew, stretched out in the small box where I had bedded down the pup. Mom had made the box for the cat to have her kittens in, but none of them had lived. And here was the small pup, sucking and pulling at the big cat with all the strength he could muster.

"It's a strange sign," Mom said. "The old cat was lonely with her kittens gone. She's happy now. The pup can stay."

I named the pup "Drum," hoping that people might think he was named for his deep mellow hound voice.

Now Drum and I would run down the path to meet Ben Puckett, I to ride the big horse's back and Drum to bark at his hoofs every step he took. Big By George stepped slowly toward our house, holding his head low as if he were trying to figure out whether Drum was just playing or figuring on biting him.

Ben Puckett was a strange, queer man. Around his neck he wore the rattles from a snake and when he turned his head the rattles shook. At our house, he stepped from the wagon and looked at my dog.

"What kind is he?" he asked.

"Hound dog!"

"Nope," he said. "He's a gin-u-wine setter dog." He shook the rattles around his neck and scared Drum half to death. "'Druther set 'round the house waitin' fer scraps than t'hunt." You could hear him laugh for a long distance.

On another trip he said, "What kind of dog did you say he was?"

"Setter dog," I answered, remembering what Ben had called him the trip before.

"Nope," said Ben. "He's a gin-u-wine sooner dog." He

shook the rattles. "Sooner set 'round the table fer scraps than t'hunt."

Ben Puckett always had a great smile on his face when he first reached the house. He chewed his dried burley leaves and amber streaked his long beard, and he didn't bother to wipe it off. Most of the stain had set in and could never be wiped off. It was easy to tell that he was no part of society. He guided the big horse along the back streets of town, passing many of the better houses on his way, gathering herbs, rags, and any odds and ends, and the big horse would be dropping piles of manure the size of a ten-gallon bucket. The people that lived close by would run out into the yards and holler at Ben, cursing him every step the big horse took. They tried to make him gather up the manure before the sun heated it and gave it to the wind and the blow flies gathered for dinner.

"Keep it!" Ben would holler back at them. "Keep it all fer yer gardens next year! Old Ben gives it t'you fer nothin' with a free heart. I had to pay fer it. Hay cost me ten cents a bale, and it comes out of my horse as fast as he can shovel it in."

"That's what's the matter with folks nowadays," Ben would say to me. "They all want their gardens fertilized without havin' to stick their hands into a manure pile to do it."

But when Ben stooped over to examine the herbs, the smile left his face. You'd have thought he would drop dead right here in our yard before he could straighten up. "Bad year fer herbs," he'd say, painfully, as if whatever had hurt the herbs had hurt him twice as bad. "Too much water in the

ground and the herbs growed too fast. No strength to 'em."
Or he'd say, "Bad year fer herbs. Dry spell has hurt 'em. All
their strength just plumb shriveled up."

According to Ben there had never been a good weather
year for herbs here in the valley. Before he finished talking
you had the feeling that if he hauled them off he'd be doing
you a great favor. He paid us very little for them.

v

June. The hot sun came, and with it the blooms of the
wild blackberry along the slopes, trailing the ridges, over
and down into the hollows. The blooms swayed in the
warm summer wind and the bees gathered for the honey,
and the humming bird stood above the vines, suspended in
air. Green snakes slid over the vines precisely enough to
miss the thorns along the way. And all the time small green-
seeded eyes were slowly pushing the blooms away and the
warm sun was slowly pulling the green from the berry,
turning it a deep purple.

Then came the Fourth of July. It had one meaning here
in the valley, so far as we Clarks were concerned: blackber-
ries were ripe. Our entire family went into the hills early of
the mornings. We started before the sun was up because
here on the slopes in July the sun can blister you through
clothing.

The grass was still dewy, the wind blew the spider
webs woven on every blade of grass, the milkweeds were
heavy with ladybugs, and the bull thistle and Queen Anne's

152

lace stuck above the broom sage. The berries would be so wet that, when we stopped to tilt our buckets, the blue water poured from the bottom. We tied smaller buckets around our waist so that we would have both hands free to pick. And we watched for the copperheads and rattlesnakes that could be found curled under the thick vines.

In the hollows the shadberry grew; some called it the dewberry. It was a large, sweet, juicy berry that you loved to slip into your mouth. The shade of the hollow made it as cool as a drink from a sweet spring. But Mom wouldn't let us eat berries in the field. Once you started eating, you wouldn't stop, and before long your stomach wouldn't hold all the berries. If you tried to sneak them into your mouth, the berry juice would lie on you every time; it stained lips and tongues purple. Each morning after we came back from the berry fields, Mom would line us up and inspect our tongues. The bluest cleaned the buckets.

We picked until the sun became unbearable, and then down the slopes we came, dreading the poke-juice remedy that Mom would put on our chigger welts. The poke-juice remedy burned like fire. I'd just as soon have kept the chiggers.

It was the job of us boys to sell some of the berries in town. Jerry and I usually ended up selling the berries, with James and Bob standing at a fair distance claiming no kin to either us or the berries.

"Never seen anyone act so highfalutin when they ain't got nothin'," Jerry said, squinting his eyes at them.

We sold the berries for fifteen cents a gallon and still no one trusted us. So we kept an empty gallon bucket with us to pour out berries and show people that the top did not hold the big berries and the bottom sun berries. But each time we emptied one bucket into another the berries settled a little farther and we had a little less.

Meanwhile our sisters were back home playing with strings of acorns they had gathered off the oaks along the ridges.

"Well, Miss Clark! Isn't that a new pearl necklace you're wearing today?"

"Lord, honey! I've had this one for years now. But this bracelet is new. Just a little something I picked up in Catlettsburg."

vi

Since Jerry's slop business had been wiped out by the move from the Leaning Tower, he became restless and searched for new ways to make money. During our first spring season along the foothills, he found a new business: picking and selling wild greens.

"Don't you see," he told me, "we can make all kinds of money. We know the wild greens, and where they grow, and all we'll need to begin with are two knives and two brown paper pokes."

We knew the wild greens, all right; I doubt if any other family here in the valley has as many specialists in wild greens as ours. Each of us had begun when we were so small that Mom had carried us to the green fields on her hip. She sat us down to play in the dirt while she gathered them.

While other babies cut their teeth on teethers, we cut our teeth on wild greens along the banks of the two rivers and other low lands of the valley. At the age of seven I could tell the difference between wild watercress, dandelion, plantain, wild sweet potato, poke, mustard, wild lettuce, mouse-ear, whitetop, dock, wild carrot tops, and all the others. Each year Mom canned what we couldn't eat right off—which wasn't much, considering that we were a family of ten. If you've ever tasted wild greens simmered in a pot of water, fried in a skillet with bacon grease, and then smothered with vinegar, you'll know what I mean.

On occasion we had sold a few of the greens, though we had actually never gathered just for selling. But now we began to dream of the money to be made by selling wild greens taller than the hills here in the valley.

So Jerry and I went out to gather greens on the bottoms along Catlettscreek. We had to hurry; the rich bottom lands here would soon be turned for crops. The sight we found along the creek was enough to make any green-picker's eyes light up. Manure from the cattle had enriched the bottoms, and wherever the greens were close to a manure pile they shot up like weeds. And if the manure piles had lain for a while and lost the strength to burn, wild greens shot right up from the middle of them.

"Look here!" I called, pointing to a big bunch of plantain in a manure pile. "Biggest pile I ever saw!" Jerry answered, moving away and working higher on the banks. When I suggested to him that he try cutting some from the manure, he turned low to the creek to gather watercress. Little chance of coming across a manure pile there. Did Jerry think I was going to do all the cutting where the smell of manure was so potent I could hardly breathe, and flies so thick that I had to shoo them away to cut the green?

"Come on up here and help me," I shouted. "We got enough watercress. Too much will make the greens strong. We need some more mouse-ear and whitetop and poke shoots."

Jerry thought a minute. "Well, I don't see any use for us both to stick our hands into the manure piles. Your hands are already dirty. I wouldn't mind if my hands were dirty. But we almost got the pokes full now."

"Then I'll cut the greens and you can wash them off in the creek," I said.

"No need in washing them," Jerry said. "We'll sell them after dark and people won't be able to see the manure."

"They can smell it."

"Not if we sell down wind."

That seemed like a good idea. Washing the greens was hard. As long as we didn't try to sell a second time to the same house, we should make out. We carried our pokes from the creek and waited around for the shadows to come to the valley.

"They ain't apt to buy the greens from me as quick as they will from you," Jerry said. "Big as I am they might think I stole the greens," he said. "And besides, me with a haircut and all, they might just think I got all kinds of money and don't need to sell the greens. So you walk right up to the houses and mess your hair up and look as sad as you can . .. like you're about starved to death. Tell 'em you're trying to buy something to eat."

After about a dozen houses, the truest words I spoke were the ones about being almost starved to death. I was ready to quit and go home and take my chances on finding something to eat there. I was tired of doing all the work. Jerry followed me to the edge of each yard and snuck his head from around a bush to watch.

"We'll try one more place," Jerry said. "If we don't sell them, we'll take them back to the creek and keep them under water until tomorrow and try again."

But when Jerry chose the last house for me to try I flatly refused. I wouldn't try to sell greens to the two Milton sisters. Both women, according to Mom, were so tight with money that they'd been afraid to get married because some of it might leak out. Both were at the top of society, and charter members of the Younger Women's Society.

"Try it," Jerry said. "Mom could have lied on them. After all, ain't they served you food in the lines at the schoolhouse? And wasn't there times that they even patted you on the head when you went through?"

They'd patted me on the head all right. But it was to mark me, so that I couldn't slip through the line again.

Finally I backed down and walked through their long yard. What Jerry didn't know was that I had noticed the small yellow roadster was missing from the driveway. If anyone came to the door, it would be Miss Minnie, their maid. She loved greens about as well as we did at our house.

Miss Minnie opened the door, and her eyes widened. "Land sakes, honey! Wild greens! Tell the truth, there's nothing finer. Ten cents for the lot."

"Well, I don't know," I answered, eyeing the two pokes. "I'll have to ask my brother."

Miss Minnie reached down into the pokes and pulled out a big bunch of plantain. "These greens ain't tough, are they?" she asked. "Seems to be a little brownness to this bunch, like it had been in the sun too long. Besides, I won't be able to give you the dime till Saturday when I get paid."

"Can't do that," Jerry said, when I returned to the bush where he was waiting. "She'll have a chance to see the manure on the greens."

"She thinks it's the sun."

"She'll know different when the wind changes."

"I'll tell her then," I said, walking back to the porch. Jerry thought I planned to tell her she'd have to pay cash, but I meant I'd tell her about the manure.

"Pays to be truthful, honey, 'deed it does," said Miss Minnie. "Little manure never hurt nobody. Water will wash it right off."

We walked toward home. I was wondering if the manure would be as hard to wash out of the greens as it had been out of the skin on my hands. Some I hadn't been able to wash out. Jerry wouldn't have this problem. His hands were as white as the moon that came to settle for the night over the valley.

CHAPTER 10

Even on the first day of school I knew the schoolhouse very well. The only difference was that it was the first time I had gone inside for anything except shelter from the flood waters. Since this had been charity, my brothers and sisters did not seem to appreciate my pointing out to everyone, even the teacher, all the places where I had at one time slept in the schoolhouse. For my own protection, I didn't mention anything about the many nights I had fought with erasers and scratched on the wooden seats and blackboards.

I wore the best clothes Mom had for me: a third-hand pair of corduroy knickers and a shirt, but no shoes. I say third-hand because they had been second-hand when Jerry wore them to school the year before. My brothers all wore knickers. And the corduroy made a screeching noise if you allowed the legs to rub when you walked, a noise which James and Bob and even Jerry did not like. It drew attention to the pants. And they were never sure that Mom hadn't bought them here in Catlettsburg. But there was an art to preventing knickers from screeching. My brothers had learned to bow their legs and walk as if they were straddling a long line of barrels.

On the big morning, my hair was slicked down with lard and Mom had pulled out the knots in my long hair until my scalp was sore. I waited for daylight to break at the schoolhouse. Getting there so early paid off: I gained the rear seat in the first grade, close to a back window. I could go out this window if the teacher came toward me. I

Second Ward school building, Catlettsburg.

"Even on the first day of school I knew the schoolhouse very well." (Author's note: Once served as both high school and grade school. It was a grade school when I grew up. I attended school for 8 years here.)

wouldn't be snatched bald-headed like the others. The teacher just might do this, my brothers had said.

Ched Littler came to the schoolhouse that morning just as daylight broke and took the seat in front of me, next farthest from the teacher's desk. Finally the class began. When the teacher looked our way, I heard Ched sniff and wipe at his nose. The teacher kept staring at him and I heard him whimper. I made ready to jump out the window. I heard a trickle on the floor and watched a pool of water form under Ched's seat. The bigger the pool grew, the more confidence I gained. I knew I wasn't the dumbest one in the first grade, anyhow. At least I had sense enough to go outside if I had to wet.

"How many can write their name?" the teacher asked a few minutes later. Only one boy got up from his seat.

"And what is your name?" the teacher asked.

"Tater," he said.

"Well, that's an odd name. Where did it come from?"

"A tater. Don't you know what a tater is?"

The teacher asked us to bring paper, pencil, and a jar of paste to school the first week. When I told Mom, she said that she'd always figured school to be a good thing, but it had become far too expensive since she was a girl. Then they had used only a slate tablet and a piece of chalk, and the school furnished both.

But the teacher had said we must have those things, and I was sure she meant just what she said. So I lay awake every night that week thinking for sure that the next day in school she'd snatch me bald-headed. I cried as low as I could, because I felt ashamed that the rest of the family might hear me. But of the morning my eyes lied on me; they were red and swollen.

Jerry at last agreed to share some of his paper after Mom promised to buy him a new pack the first of the week. She gave me a pencil herself and toward the end of the week she mixed me a jar of paste, using white baking flour and water.

"This is as good as you give a nickel for at the store," Mom said. "If the paste hardens up, just add a little more water to it and stir." The rest of the family was ashamed of the flour paste. It was a sign of poverty. They gathered real paste jars, used, from the trash cans at school and hid the flour paste inside. I preferred the fruit jar; it was the biggest. If I ever learned to spell paste, I would label my jar.

During the first week of school, I concentrated most on learning to write out my full name, a feat harder than dog-paddling the Big Sandy. "I'll write out the letters for you," the teacher said one afternoon. "You take the paper home and study the letters. While you're at it, tell your mother not to put lard on your hair. It'll thin out from the heat at school and run down your face. Lard is bad for the scalp."

I practiced writing my name until my hand cramped. And finally I could write BILLIE without looking at the paper. "You're silly," my sister Margaret said to me. "BILLIE is the way you spell a girl's name."

The blood came to my face. I had been accused of being a girl before. This time I went straight to Mom.

"And that woman is supposed to be a school teacher!" Mom said.

I tore the paper into pieces, divided up the pieces and

tore them again. With each tear I hated the teacher more.

"Let me show you," Mom said. "Here's the way to write it." I watched her, wondering why she hadn't shown me before. For that matter, why wasn't Mom teaching school herself?

ii

In the spring, the rains came and the sky was covered with clouds as black as the wings of crows. Day was almost the same as night, lit like the dim beam of worn-out flashlight batteries. The rains wet the ground so deep down that we could not turn the garden in the back yard. The creek swelled and the long bottoms were under water, the tops of old corn stalks quivering in the muddy currents; birds lit upon the stalks and searched the water for bugs. People talked about their potato seeds rotting in the ground.

The rains lasted long into the summer and knocked the blooms from the wild berry vines and from the fruit trees. The two rivers rose and fell—up and down like the sides of a dying horse. People paid little attention to the mood of the rivers; they didn't worry about the rivers flooding of the summer. Many years had taught them that January, February, and March were the flood months. Only Dad mentioned that floods are long in coming; they grow like small tree sprouts.

"Never seen rains stay this long here in the valley since 1913," Dad said. That had been the year of the worst flood the valley had ever known. Dad said that the water from the hills would not all drain back to the rivers. There would be too much, and more yet to come.

Winter, and the snows came. They began early and were the deepest that Dad could remember. When the earth thawed under warmer weather, the water started moving slowly back to the rivers. Mountain springs pushed up out of the earth and feeder streams trailed out of their banks, unable to hold the water.

The rivers swelled. So many people gathered along the

Billy C. Clark's father in his shoe shop in Catlettsburg. Photo courtesy of Billy C. Clark.

"Since 1913 I've worked to keep a shoe shop in Catlettsburg where I could work for myself. From 1913 till 1937 is a long time."

banks that it was hard to find a place to stand and look at the muddy rivers. But what you couldn't see you could hear. The currents hummed like motors; then one day they stopped and a quietness came over the town.

"The water will cover the valley," Dad said. "Since 1913 I've worked to keep me a shoe shop in Catlettsburg where I could work for myself. I'm afraid I'll lose it this year. From 1913 till 1937 is a long time." And he looked off toward the two rivers.

Rains came again—cold wintry rains that froze along the limbs of the trees at night and melted when the sun came in the day. The rivers moved over the banks and school was dismissed.

"We can thank the Lord that this time we are on high ground," Mom said, and set about making room in our basement for those who would be crowded out of the schoolhouse.

The rivers came on. People moved like bees around a hive. They hauled their things across town, in cars, trucks, wagons and on their backs. In front and behind them came the river rats, hundreds of them. Each day they became less concerned about cover and walked out in the open ahead of the rising waters—great brown river rats the size of half-grown cats, their hair covered and plastered by river muck. We fought them with clubs, rocks, or anything else that we could find to throw. They stood on their hind legs to fight us, fearing the rivers more than people. From the top of the ridge above our house you could look over the town and see nothing but water. Men oared boats over the tops of the tallest buildings.

I sneaked to the schoolyard where great gatherings of people met each night to hold church and to pray. The first few nights they prayed for their homes to stand against the water. But when black clouds appeared again and word came that the clouds were blacker up river, they prayed for their souls. They begged the Lord to take the bulge out of the rivers. People popped up from the crowds like popcorn in a pot and stood in the open to confess past wrongs, and some sniggered from the sidelines as they talked.

"I knowed old Liz Tarpin was runnin' round. Tuck a flood to git it out of'r."

"Knowed Bill Lucas didn't make money enough cuttin' timber to drive a car like he's got. Thought he was workin' moonshine but couldn't be sure till the waters come."

"Stolt that hog twenty years ago come Saturday."

"Twenty years ago! Can you imagine? They ain't a law in the land can touch him fer't now."

"Look at old Ben Liles over there in the center of the ring. You'd think he were runnin' fer governor the way he's shakin' hands and carryin' on. Makin' amends. First he was constable, then moved on to justice of the peace, a justice of the peace that knew about as much law as a cross-eyed woodpecker. I knowed all the time he was takin' money and turnin' nothin' in to the higher courts. Watch him eye the rivers, twitchin'. If they drop one inch he'll close up like a snappin' turtle and try to prosecute the first man that reminds him of his wrongs."

Some mocked the rivers: "I'll go to the tops of the mountains before I'll stand in a crowd and make laughin' stock of myself."

"What if the rivers comes that high?"

"I've got a hell of a lot to tell them."

Mom said, "Wickedness! Wickedness! The Lord has come to make people repent. Oh Lord!" Mom dropped to her knees and slowly called the names of every salesman that had visited our house trying to collect for his wares. She repented every trip to a fortuneteller.

The rivers crawled into the basement under our house. It washed against the foot of the hills, the farthest it had ever come. The tall hills became islands.

"The world is coming to an end!" people shouted, dropping to their knees and praying harder than ever before.

"It was two hogs I stolt twenty years ago, Lord, instead of one like I said in the first place."

"Watch the water! If it comes an inch, he'll raise the anny."

"Oh Lord, the money I've took!" Ben Liles said.

I still had trouble writing my full name. What if the world came to an end and when I reached Heaven I couldn't remember well enough to write my name in the Book that Jerry said was there for all to sign? I was too scared to practice now. Would the Lord know that I hadn't been in school long and hadn't had much time to practice? I cried with the rest.

People suffered from hunger. The rivers had come so fast that little food had been saved from the stores in town. Most of the owners had remained open until the last minute trying to make a little more money. And this last minute had cost them. Now men oared joeboats over the town, stopping where they judged a store to be beneath them. They gouged into the water with long poles, hoping to break out the store windows so that food might float to the surface.

Lines formed again at the small schoolhouse. I went there to eat. They gave hardly enough to keep our stomachs from cramping. But it was not hard to take when the person's stomach next to you growled louder than yours and drowned out the sound.

One morning a path of light appeared in the sky. People gathered to stare at it. They dropped to their knees and prayed again. "The rivers have crested," they cried, wiping tears away.

iii

Along the foot of the hills, less than a half mile from our house, a relief shack was built and people gathered in long lines each day to get food. Early of the mornings Jerry and I stood in line, Jerry holding a sack and me a gallon jug. We got tired of standing in the long line and usually we cut over the hills and tried to come out ahead of the line, snitching a place when someone wasn't looking, or taking advantage of an old man with time-fog over his eyes. There was a great advantage in being up front. First come first served, and commodities such as bacon lasted only a short time.

Come hell or high water you could always depend on one thing: grapefruit. At our house we ate them raw, cooked, baked, boiled and roasted. They always came out the same: grapefruit.

Each morning before we left the house Mom would frown and offer a prayer. It was not that she was showing ungratefulness, she said, but she prayed that we would bring back something besides grapefruit. She said she did not believe the good Lord intended for people here in the valley to eat nothing but grapefruit. If so, He would have sprouted them on the limbs of the trees around here.

And even now jokesters were to be found. Slim Mullins would walk up and down the line swinging a rope in his hands.

"What's the need for a rope today, Slim?"

"Hell, ain't you heard? They're given' away whole hogs today!"

"Whole hogs! Lord God! Hold my place, Mert, whilst I run home fer a pushcart!"

Just above the relief shack, another wooden hut had been built. And this hut was the reason for the gallon jug in my hands. Inside this hut men made great pots of vegetable soup. Each family was allowed one jug a day, furnishing their own jug. Near one end of the hut a long bench table had been built. Soup was served to people whose houses were under water and men dealt out bowls of steaming hot soup to people along the table like cards over a poker table over on Bloody Front.

When Jerry reached the near end of the line I would sneak away. He saw me each day and he shook his fist and threatened me back. He knew he would lose his place in the line if he came after me.

"You live out of the flood?" the server would say.

"Nope," I would answer.

"House under water?"

"Out of sight."

He eyed me with suspicion and set down a bowl for me. I drank the soup and then went to the bushes for my jug and got it filled at the hut.

I didn't really mind at all carrying the jug of hot soup home. But I will say that cutting through the hills made it a hard trip. You try walking the sides of the hills with a hot jug in your hands, your feet tangling in honeysuckle and saw briers, and now and then a slender branch of a blackberry vine reaching out to snatch you across the face. It never seemed right that I should have to carry it around the hills. I did it because Jerry was ashamed to be seen with the

Division Street during the flood of 1913, Catlettsburg.

"The rivers fell and then stopped."

burlap sack over his shoulder. I was proud to carry the jug, and mad that no one ever got to see me carrying it home.

iv

When the rivers began to fall, people gathered there cursing them. "Damned rivers! Hell of a thing for a man to have to put up with!"

Before, the same people had dropped to their knees and prayed.

The rivers fell and then stopped. And for days they remained at a standstill. People stopped cursing. They stood in silence and watched, a prayer and a curse ready to race off their tongues, depending on whether the rivers came or went. A foot rise and they were on their knees; a foot drop and the dictionary wouldn't hold such words.

The rivers fell and people came with shovels and sticks to scrape the muck back into the falling waters, cursing every step they took.

In most places along the streets of town, the mud had caked and the wind had hardened it until it remained a foot deep. Work was easy to find now. My brothers worked scraping muck from inside buildings. They worked inside the buildings wading a foot or more of water. They used poles and mattocks, breaking the muck loose from the walls and floors, stirring it into soup and pushing it out with river water. Once the water was out of the building, they built fires inside to dry out the timbers of the old buildings. Soon the wind and sun would bow the old buildings out like nail kegs.

171

I was too small for much besides gathering driftwood. I had worked for a while with my brothers scraping muck, but I quit when the owners refused to pay me along with my brothers. For some reason they considered me a toss-in when they hired my brothers for a job. Gathering driftwood allowed me to work by myself.

Between loads of driftwood I chased rats back across town. They had came back out of the hills and high lands on their way to the rivers. I ran them to the muddy banks, down through the slime where they bogged down, and then knocked them in the head with clubs.

Dad had lost practically everything he owned to the flood. His larger pieces of shoe machinery, which he had not been able to haul out of the basement, were all but ruined.

Front Street during the 1913 flood, Catlettsburg.

"I was too small for much besides gathering driftwood."

CHAPTER 11

I was standing in the schoolhouse yard, where the snow was almost a foot deep. The wind picked up the dry flakes on top of the crust and whipped them into my face as if it were mad at me. I was trying to keep my feet warm until school began, at least a half hour away, by kicking them against a tree. "Are those the only shoes you have to wear?" the teacher asked as she walked across the schoolhouse yard.

The sole on the right shoe was loose and the snow had caked under it, forming a lump that caused me to walk with a limp. It would take a stick to pry it out and a few more steps in the snow would bring it back.

"Why, your feet are almost out on the naked snow," she exclaimed.

I kicked around at the heavy crust of the snow. "If Mom crosses the river this Saturday, she's going to try to find me another pair."

"You poor little thing."

"You ought to see the shoes that my brother Jerry's wearing," I said. "When I got his he got James's, and Mom says that James has the biggest feet of any boy his size in the valley. Took big feet from Grandpa Hewlett."

Two days later when I came home from school Mom was all smiles. A large box was in front of her and inside the box were two pairs of brogans, one pair for me and one pair for Jerry.

They weren't ordinary brogans, to be sure. Across the

Center Street during the flood of 1913.

"The Ohio and the Big Sandy were restless rivers, moving out of their banks at least every other year."

toes were large metal plates, and on the heels and tips of the toes small hobnails stuck out like buck teeth. The teeth would dig into the earth and give you a solid footing.

Jerry frowned when Mom asked him to try on the brogans for size. He was about the most ungrateful person I'd ever known when it came to wearing shoes like these. Dad was the same as Jerry. When he came home and saw the brogans he asked, "Where did they come from?"

"They came from relief," Mom said. "Billy's teacher recommended them."

"Take them back!" Dad shouted, and for the first time I saw fury in his eyes. "I may be poor, but I ain't taking handouts from them people. Not while I'm able to work!"

Mom began to cry.

But later that night after we'd all gone to bed I heard Dad say to her, "All right, Bert. I know they need shoes. I worry about it all the time. It would take a long time to buy them."

"The weather is cold," said Mom.

"There's good leather in those shoes," Dad agreed.

I was happier than ever about the brogans. They were better shoes than I had thought. Dad knew his leather.

Before the week was out I learned we weren't the only boys at the schoolhouse that had them. Sid Taylor had a pair and they were so new that the leather smelled inside the schoolroom. And his older brother Hyford had a pair, too. Both Jerry and Hyford felt they were above wearing the brogans. So they had scuffed the new leather with rocks until the shoes looked like they'd been worn on two battle-fields before the government had decided to release them.

Then Jerry sneaked a file from Dad's basement and he and Hyford filed the hobs off, to keep from sounding like a team of shod horses across the boards of the schoolhouse floor.

I was proud of my brogans. I especially liked the silver plate across the toes. You could slide the steel toe against the side of a rock and send out sparks for two feet ahead. As Jerry and I walked to school, I sparked every rock in the path and for a good-sized rock I left the path. I'd rear back with my foot and the sound of the steel against rock would carry for a long distance in the quiet of morning. Jerry would frown and squint his eyes toward the schoolhouse yard, sure that everyone there had heard the sound.

If I found a flat rock along the path, I would step on top of it and scrape, and the sound would drift out like pulling a corncob over a washboard. I stepped on leaves and paper until so much gathered on the hobs that I had to stop and tear them loose.

Finally Jerry said to Mom one evening, "Either make him stop sparking rocks and picking up leaves and paper or make him take off the steel plates and hobs."

"They're my shoes," I insisted, brushing the brogans to keep the leather looking new.

"Don't you spark the rocks on purpose," said Mom. "You'll wear out the shoes."

Now Jerry walked ahead of me on school mornings, far ahead. He pretended he didn't hear the sound of the plates over the rocks. Tap, tap, tap, tap! You wouldn't have thought he was with me at all.

"What do you suppose the line is for?" Sid Taylor said to me one morning as we walked into the schoolroom. Instead of taking seats, everyone had formed a line around the back of the room. The teacher motioned me and Sid to the end of the line.

I peeked around to see what was taking place. A woman in a white uniform was bending John Siples' head toward the light coming in the window. She ruffled his hair like feathers on a chicken, said something to the teacher, and John took his seat. Like knocking crows off a fence, the line shortened. Then the woman pulled my head over and tried to part my hair.

"This one," she said to the teacher. The next thing I knew I was on my way upstairs to the principal's office.

Now, you were sent to the principal's office only when you had done something wrong, like the time Jerry's teacher had caught him spitting tobacco juice in the flower pots at school and wilting down the flowers. The teacher had spent a good deal of money on insecticides of all sorts trying to cure the wilt. There had been none powerful enough to deal with ambeer except the long flat paddle with the holes bored in the end of it that the principal had used on Jerry's rump. Jerry had never mentioned this at home.

As I entered the principal's office, I saw a small table, and on the table were half-gallon jugs filled with a white liquid. The principal reached for a jug.

"Take this and go straight home!" he said. "Carry this

note with you. Your mother is to pour the coal oil on your head until you are rid of them. Cutting some of your hair away wouldn't hurt you either!"

Mom took the cork off the jug and smelled.

"It's coal oil all right," she said. She pulled my head over her lap and parted my hair. "Eaten up with lice, I'll tell you!"

You can find the definition of a louse in any dictionary, but if you don't know what it is like to have them, I can tell you: You may well not know that you are packing them around until you're told. And then they become as thick in your mind as grains of sand along the riverbanks. Your head begins to itch and you can't scratch enough. Now that I knew what and where they were, I could hardly hold my head still in Mom's lap. She clamped her knees around my head in a scissor hold. I thought of what the principal had said about cutting my hair, but I wouldn't tell her this. How would you like to go to school with a bowl haircut?

Mom poured the coal oil over my hair and it ran down my face, into my eyes and burned like fire. I felt it seep into the corners of my mouth and I thought I'd drown before she let me up for air.

For two days I stayed home from school and three times daily Mom doused me good with the oil. And toward the end of week I went back to school. Another jug of oil and I was on my way home again. My lice were mighty stubborn.

The smell of coal oil is rank, and now that everyone knew what the oil was for they began to shame me. "Don't strike a match close to him!" they shouted. "He'll go up like a blow torch!"

"There ought to be another school just for trash to go to, that's what Mother says."

I became lonesome at school now. Even Sid Taylor wouldn't get near me. Mom claimed I had caught the bugs from him and his mother claimed that he had caught the bugs from me. Where they had come from to begin with, no one said.

Bigger boys cornered me at school and poked at me with sticks like you'd poke a dog. They laughed and shouted and if I ran toward them to fight they ran from me and shouted, "Watch the bugs!" If I could have tackled one of them, I planned to rub our heads together in hopes that some of the bugs would transfer to another freight line.

"Teacher's gonna send you home
Cause little cooties like to roam."

"I don't know where they come from!" Mom exclaimed. "You don't believe they're coming from that infernal dog?"

"I know where," said Jerry. "From the trash he plays with at school!"

Mom was on her feet. "Don't you ever use the word 'trash' again when you speak of people!" she shouted.

"Well, his hair's too long to find the bugs," Jerry said, his own hair hanging like a girl's bangs, fresh from a new bowl haircut.

Within minutes I was in the back yard with my head over a barrel, and Mom shaved me until I had about as much hair left as a cucumber.

But I got even with Jerry the next day. "Mom I've got

something to tell," I said as I came in from school. She was scrubbing clothes and did not look up.

"The teacher got Jerry," I said.

"Bugs!" said Mom.

"No, the teacher caught him spitting tobacco juice in the flower pots and wilting down the flowers."

"Tobacco juice!" And when he returned Jerry got a licking! "I'm too big to be whipped now," he said to me that night. "I'm leaving home!" He moved around the room packing his clothes into a small bundle, and swung them over his shoulder and walked quietly down the stairs. I heard the door open to the outside and tears came to my eyes. I was sorry that I'd tattled on him. The wind whistled in the trees along the slopes and the birds were restless under the eaves of the roof. The mournful sound of an owl drifted down the sides of the slopes. Then I heard footsteps on the stairs again. Something came toward the bed.

"Move over. I think I'll wait until daylight," Jerry said.

The next morning I told the teacher that we all slept in the same bed at our house, and she sent us all home. She knew that lice have a wanderer's foot.

iii

The Ohio and the Big Sandy were restless rivers, moving out of their banks at least every other year. But both were as calm as a summer breeze compared to Mom's restlessness once she was away from their banks. During the seven years from 1936 to 1943 we moved a total of

Billy C. Clark working his trapline in and around Catlettsburg, 1956.
Photos courtesy of Billy C. Clark.

"The fourteen miles each morning before class, over snags, drifts, rocks, logs, and mud, was a long distance to walk."

fourteen times. Twice a year we would trade houses with Mrs. Larker, a neighbor who lived around the side of the hill about a hundred and fifty yards away.

"How much time have we got?" Dad would ask when spring came.

Mom would say, "Well, I told Mrs. Larker she could bring her things whenever she wanted. I know that big house gets lonely for her now that all but three of the children are gone. It's too much room."

Mrs. Larker would be coming around the bend with a load even while Mom was talking. We began packing and carrying. Our clothing was tied in bed sheets with Mom cautioning us to keep the sheets off the ground. We staggered up the path, and traveled it so many times it became as clear and slick as a muskrat slide.

We met the Larkers coming and going. And we cursed the rivers for the work they had brought by giving up drift furniture. When the hot sun was overhead Mom would go up the path carrying a chair. She met Mrs. Larker, who by a strange coincidence was carrying a chair too. Each scooted their chair off the path under the shade of the trees and discussed the pain of moving. They could only "sit a little while." But oh how the little whiles grew to be big! We passed them for the rest of the day.

I had a snapping turtle which I had caught from Catlettscreek and put in a bucket of slop. But he was a restless turtle, traipsing off all the time. I honestly believe that we moved so much he never really got to know where his home was.

He preferred Mrs. Larker's big house, and for good

reason. Close to her front door, a natural spring bubbled out of the earth, and here he had room to stretch out and swim, which I figured was what a turtle was supposed to do.

Growing was his biggest mistake. Soon he could reach his long neck from the spring and snap a fly out of the air. He was getting dangerous. "You'll have to take that turtle back to the creek!" Mom finally said, and to satisfy her I took him as far as the spring. I tried to tell him that to stick his head out of the spring when someone was in sight was to be served with an eviction notice. But did you ever try to reason with a turtle? That evening he really did take a fair chunk from my sister Mary's leg. Hoping to get the drop on her, I ran into the house. "Mom! Mom! My turtle's come back from the creek!"

"I'm surprised that you're just now finding out," Mom said. "He returned a few minutes after you took him back to the creek."

With nine different kinds of meat in a turtle how could I know that it wasn't chicken stew we ate the next evening? That's what Mom said and what I believed till I counted our chickens.

Fall, and we moved again.

"Lord, it's a hot day, Mrs. Larker!"

"One of the hottest of the year, Mrs. Clark!"

"Hope you won't think I'm a dirty housekeeper, Mrs. Larker. Once I get settled, I intend to come down and straighten up a little better."

"Don't you worry about that, Mrs. Clark. I swear! Don't see how so much dirt could accumulate so quickly. It makes me ashamed for you to see the house this way."

"I kept trying to get Mason to fix that leak over the kitchen roof, Mrs. Larker. Lord knows I tried! You know, the place it was leaking this spring."

"Well, you'll find the old chicken house is no better. I tried to get Mr. Larker to cut the weeds and vines before they pulled over the fence. But with no chickens of our own, he never goes up there ... 'Spect we better move the chairs back a little. Mr. Larker almost hit me with his end of the bed post. Never watches where he's going!"

iv

We had found an old hen in our lot when we moved from the Leaning Tower to the foothills. She had a brood of ten chicks which she gathered every night on the low limbs of the oaks. Dad built a small pen at the side of the house, clipped the chickens' wings, and took away their freedom. Each of us claimed a chicken and named it; I claimed the only rooster in the lot. He'd been hatched out with a crooked leg, and I named him Jephtha after my great-grandpa Jephtha Bonaparte Hewlett. He walked to one side like a dog will do at a fast pace. And around the lot he went each day, drooping his wings, losing his balance and falling to the ground. But he never gave up. He got back on his feet and courted the hens again.

"Watch that rooster close," James said to me. "He's old enough now to lay. He'll lay a square egg."

"But how'd he get it out?" I asked.

"Easy," James said. "He ain't round in the back like a

hen. He's square." But if he was, you never could have told it by feeling. "He'll crow after the egg comes out."

For a whole livelong summer I followed that rooster. All he did was crow. If each crow meant an egg, I could have gathered them up in a bushel basket.

"Don't mean an egg every time he crows," James said. "Only when he crows the loudest."

I kept following him. Still no egg.

"Maybe he's laying somewhere in the hills," James said. And it was true Jephtha wandered out of the lot during the day.

"I've searched there," I answered. My back was sore from pulling honeysuckle vines apart and bending to crawl under blackberry vines.

"But have you looked along the foot of the hills?" James asked.

"Yes."

"Well, when he lays he'll lay high on the hills where no one can see him. And a square egg won't roll down hill."

Later I told Mom about a rooster laying a square egg, and she frowned. "James is kidding you," she said. "A rooster can't lay an egg. Not even a round one."

Yet I never really knew why he couldn't.

v

"What you doin' way up here on top of the ridge after dark, boy?" Bardrock Shinley said to me.

Bardrock was a small, short man—thin, with long

arms that dangled out in front of him like they were loose at the joints. His chin was pointed and his face as pale as a coal miner's.

"Trying to catch a possum," I answered.

"Any luck?"

"Nope."

"Don't look like much of a dog you got there."

He stared down at Drum who had come in to see what it was all about. Drum looked at Bardrock and whined.

"He's a good dog," I said.

"Some curs are."

Bardrock's shirt bulged at the front and a sound came from his bibbed overalls. It was a low cluck like a chicken will make quarreling of the night. He grabbed at the front of his shirt, and the next thing I knew he was holding the long neck of a chicken that had peeped out of the front. Drum hunkered and shamed me by growling low, from deep down in his throat.

"Doin' a little huntin' myself," Bardrock said. "Caught one wild chicken already."

"Wild!" I said.

"Lots of wild chickens here in these parts."

"Gosh, I never knew that."

"Not many others do either," he said. "Reckon that's the reason I'm about the only one who catches them. Whose boy are you?"

"Mason Clark's."

"Well, damn, I knowed Mason for years. Best fiddler in the country. More he drinks the faster he plays."

I frowned. "Dad don't drink!"

"Well, reckon a frog don't swim either. Huh?"

He looked back over his shoulder. "Bet you could shinny up a tree in a hurry," he said.

He rolled a cigarette and put a match to it. "Wouldn't want to catch a chicken or two, would you?"

My heart beat fast. Once I learned where and how to catch wild chickens I could tell Jerry and we could come back and make ourselves a killing.

"Yes," I said.

"Can you run that cur home?" he asked.

"I can try," I said.

"Then put the skids to 'im," he said.

At first I tried a switch. Drum rolled over willing to take a whipping and looked up at me with his sad eyes. I picked him up and set him on his feet again. And he walked off a piece in the bushes, stopped, and looked back at me as if he thought I couldn't see him.

As we walked out the ridge, Bardrock talked to me about the chickens. Now and then I would glance back and see Drum sneaking along after us. He stopped when we did and walked only when we did.

The wild chickens, according to Bardrock, roosted in the trees low on the slopes. This did not seem uncommon to me. Most of the people that owned chickens here along the slopes of the hills let them roost in the trees. Out the ridge a piece, we cut over the side of the hill and moved closer to the houses.

"You shinny up the tree and snatch the first chicken that you can reach by the neck. If it cackles, it'll warn the others, so hold the neck tight. Not tight enough to kill it, though. You can ease up now and then to give it air. I'll wait for you under the tree."

Bardrock motioned for me to hunker and he went ahead to take a look. "They're there all right," he said. "A limb full of 'em." I looked over a knoll and saw the chickens, roosting on a walnut tree in the bright moonlight. You could see that they were asleep on the limb, their heads tucked under their wings. They were awful close to the house on the side of the hill, it seemed to me.

"What makes you think they're wild chickens?" I asked.

"They're wild all right," Bardrock said. "Wild enough for me."

"Why are they roosting so close to the house?" I asked.

"Foxes," he said. "Them chickens got sense enough to know that foxes ain't apt to come so close to a house."

It seemed to me that if the chickens were smart enough to know that, they ought to have sense enough to know that a fox can't climb a tree. I was scared, but I sneaked across the knoll and when I looked back Bardrock motioned me up the tree. I shinnied up and grabbed the first chicken and began to slide down. I squeezed the chicken hard, and it went limp. Thinking I had killed it, I let up on my grip. Just then a cackle came from the chicken. I slipped, and the chicken went flying through the air. Lights went on all over the house and I heard the door slam. "Don't run or I'll blow your head off!" a voice yelled.

I hit the ground fast enough to outrun a 'coon. And the tree limbs hit my face and brought tears to my eyes.

I did not get caught. And neither did Bardrock—not

that night anyway. But he had been arrested many times, I found out later, and one of those times he had earned his name. This is how it happened:

One night when Bardrock had been caught he was taken to the judge's home. His shirt was puffed out like a balloon full of air.

"What have you got to say for yourself?" the judge asked.

"Not guilty," Bardrock answered.

"Then what do you have inside your shirt?"

"Rocks."

"I'm going to ask you once again. If you lie to me this time, I'll keep you in jail long enough to dry you up. What's inside your shirt?"

"Rocks."

"You've had your chance. Search him, constable." They opened Bardrock's shirt, and the chickens went every which way.

"I told you the truth, Your Honor," Bardrock said. "They're rocks: Barred Rock."

"Six months for stealing," said the judge. "Reduce it to three months for telling the truth the first time in his life."

Taking a break from working in the fields.
Photo courtesy of Earl Palmer.

CHAPTER 12

Nick Carter was three years older than I and one grade behind me in school. He wasn't dumb; he'd just missed so much schooling along the way. Nick was old enough to be independent, and he always had a little money in his pocket. His hair was long and matted, his clothes torn and patched and carrying an odor of manure. The cuffs of his shirt were as black as earth in the lowlands. People laughed at him in school and said that you should not get down wind from Nick.

Nick just didn't care. You could laugh all you wanted, and he wouldn't get mad. He'd laugh with you.

As long as I had known him, he'd been working in the creek bottoms for Melvin Hickey. It was Nick who got me my job there. I used to sit along the banks and listen to him shout at a team of mules he was working, "Gee, you sons of bitches! Haw, you bastards!" And he'd take a leather strap and swarp the big mules across the rumps and say, "Don't you fart on me!"

Down the rich bottoms he'd go, laying off furrows as straight as a sourwood sprout. At school he couldn't draw a straight line on paper to save him. But when it came to handling mules, he knew all the tricks of the trade. He worked the same mules in the same bottoms that his father and his father's father before him had worked. He knew that you had to let a mule know who was boss.

I watched him as he turned at the end of the stretch of level land and came back. The doubletree would be bouncing up and down and the trace chains clacking, and he'd stop the mules under a shade tree near the creek and let them stand. He'd chase away the horseflies and pet the big mules and speak soft words to them. While they nibbled at the tops of the tender horseweeds here in the shade, he knelt at the creek, blew away the scum from the surface, and got him a drink. It didn't matter to Nick that sewers emptied into the creek.

"Here," he'd say. "Take the mules and turn a couple of furrows. Remember, now, you got to cuss a mule when it's working and pet it when it ain't."

And down the field I'd go, holding the layoff plow so that the point would go no deeper than it had in the furrow to my left, turned by Nick. The mules would balk as soon as they found out that Nick didn't have them, and I'd look back over my shoulder toward him and he'd yell, "Cuss 'em!"

"Gee, you sons of bitches! Haw, you bastards! Git up now! Don't fart on me!" And Nick would stretch his back against a tree to scratch it and laugh for all that was in him.

"Ever notice," he said to me one day, "that a mule man holds his head to one side, whether he's working mules or walking the streets of town? Know the reason?"

"No," I answered.

"From dodging farts," Nick said, and he laughed loud enough to be heard all over the banks of the creek.

Every time I thought I could catch Nick not looking, I'd steal a glance to see if his head was tilted. To be truthful, I think Nick always knew I was peeking at him, and he'd walk around with his head tilted. A hell of a thing, I thought, to go traipsing around town with your head tilted, and people sniggering, knowing it got that way from dodging mule farts!

What Nick didn't learn from his school books, he knew from the hills and rivers of his own country. He came from a long line of fox hunters. Hard work since he had been big enough to hold a gooseneck hoe and using hay forks and plows had made him strong and muscular. Not tall, but squatty and broad. Everyone at school enjoyed Nick's good nature.

When the cold weather first began to break, he shed his shoes and walked two miles to school barefoot. He didn't care who laughed at his dirty calloused feet. He wore a little more when the snows were over the valley. He was tough as a pine knot. Lice meant nothing to him. He laughed when the principal gave him a jug of oil; he was glad to get it. "Pa says if I can keep the bugs alive and crawling, he'll never have to buy any more lamp oil."

You had to get up early to be ahead of Nick in the relief line, or any other line for that matter if they were giving away something to eat.

Plowing the creek bottoms was hard work, but neither of us went hungry while we worked. We found our lunch right there at the creek. We'd trap out a few fat minnows and crawdads and roast them over a fire. For dessert we walked higher on the creek banks and ate wild carrots.

I didn't make as much money as Nick. He handled the mules better, far surpassing me with his ability to curse. I think this was because I could never set my mind to cursing. I didn't like the words when I was a boy, and I did not use them when I became a man.

ii

Being a friend of Nick's opened up another way for me to make money. On weekend nights of the summers, and often into the winters, I went with Nick to work at the rooster pits. Here in the valley many people lived, fought, and were killed because of the roosters.

Melvin Hickey's place set off to the right as you went up creek, deep into a hollow. You got to it by traveling a dirt road. Halfway up you came to a bridge that crossed a small stream. The bridge was made of two large black oak logs. The logs challenged even a sober driver to take a car across. Drunks seldom made it, so Melvin's mules towed them out at a fair price.

The place where the chickens were fought was a large barn of rough unpainted oak, flat-roofed and covered with shingles that the wind played with. It had been built for one purpose: cock fighting.

Inside the barn, directly in the center, green oak boards formed a ring two feet high. Around this, seats had been built, reaching almost to the top of the barn. At any place along the seats, there was an open view into the pit below. The bottom of the pit was covered with sawdust.

By the door at the far end of the barn was a long, narrow box, resembling a tobacco bed box. This was known as the walk pit, or the drag pit. The owner walked his rooster in it to limber him up before he went into the larger pit to fight

194

for keeps. Later during the night, it would become a drag pit—the bloodiest of all pits. Fights were held there without handlers, so it was thought to be the really true test for a game chicken.

Game-rooster breeding was a highly specialized field, as much so as the breeding of the race horses that ran in the other end of the state. The training was just as cautious and exacting—probably more so. You could win with a rooster bred and handled by a man without a first-grade education, or by a college graduate. Each had learned his trade from the dead roosters he had carried from the pits.

There were many breeds of roosters in the valley, but the best were: the Warhorse, a big, black bird with a lot of power and a heart to match; the Allen Roundhead, a small red bird that was extremely fast; and the Dom, a bulky rooster that won his fights from sheer power and size. Breeding was a long, slow process of mixing these three, stirring them to make the perfect blend.

When you had the right combination, you picked the strongest rooster chick from the brood. You didn't hurry the young rooster you had chosen. When he became a stag you trimmed his comb and spurs, and then you turned him loose to run the hills with hens. Here he would gain strength in his legs and wind in his lungs.

When he reached his full size, you brought him from the hills to condition him for his first fight. The exercises were regular and frequent. The rooster was placed in front of you, looking away. You grabbed him by the tail and pulled backwards so fast that his feet wouldn't keep up. At first he'd go sprawling to the ground. But soon his feet would move so fast backwards that you couldn't pull him off balance. This built up his legs and taught him to back fast without turning, because once he was in the pits facing another rooster, turning was death. Next, the rooster was grabbed under the breast and flipped high into the air so he turned a complete somersault. In a few weeks he'd land on his feet better than a cat. Backward, forward, to the right, to the left—one couldn't throw him off balance.

And now the rooster was ready for his first practice fight. You matched him with an old rooster that he could handle easily, so he would gain confidence in himself. To the spurs of each were attached small boxing gloves. With these, the roosters could hit but not cut. The only blood shed would be from pecking the combs.

The rounds lasted no more than twenty seconds. While they sparred, the young rooster was watched closely. If he fought striking up from the ground, he would use a jagger gaff. The end of the jagger was tilted sharply so that when it came up it would cut deep. But suppose he liked to strike from the air. In this case the curved gaff would be used—a longer gaff that tapered very slightly at the ends.

The young rooster was turned loose to roam the hills once more. His water supply was watched closely. Not too much; not too little. Too much and he would become sick in the pit. Too little and he would become a "dry chicken," and a dullness would come to his feathers.

When he was ready for his first fight, he was weighed on the scales that hung from the oak beam at Melvin Hickey's. No rooster could be spotted more than two ounces either way. You placed your bet according to your faith in the rooster and the handler. Faith could run mighty high here at Melvin Hickey's.

Roosters were usually handled by professional handlers, because most owners didn't have the stomach for it. The two handlers stepped inside the pit with the matched roosters, allowed them to peck, and released them. Once loose, the roosters fought until one was dead. Often the birds got "coupled together"—that is, one would hang his gaffs into the other, unable to pull them free. Then a handler would uncouple them, and he was allowed from fifteen to twenty seconds to get the gaffed rooster into fighting condition again.

A good handler could "bring a rooster back." When a bird was rattled by a hard blow and bleeding from the bill, a handler thought nothing of sticking the bill into his mouth and sucking out the blood to clear the rooster's throat. Or he would put his mouth over the bird's rear and blow air up him, careful not to suck in. This gave him an extra spurt of life, it was believed. A good handler would also chew on the comb of a rooster to add more fire to him.

Melvin Hickey paid Nick and me five cents apiece to dry-pick the dead birds. Owners seldom wanted the dead roosters, so they became the property of Melvin Hickey, and the next day they would be taken to the poultry house in town. If they had been cut too badly, they were sold to restaurants for chicken salad. What if the members of the Younger Women's Society had known, as they ate their salads, that I had picked this very chicken beside the pit, smoke so heavy that I could hardly tell feather from chicken, the smell of whiskey enough to make you drunk.

Fights lasted from Friday until Monday, and I went home only long enough to let Mom know that I was alive.

People gathered around the pits until it was hard to move: both society folks and tramps; from city officials down to members of the Street Department. Women, too!

When Bloody Front closed up at night, the people there drifted out to Melvin Hickey's place. Some brought whiskey with them; others bought it at the barn—from moonshine to bottled in bond. Men and women loved, drank, and fought. Often during the nights they staggered up the sapling ladder to the hay-filled attic. Small strains of hay dribbled through the cracks beneath them, and sometimes they lost money that Nick and I searched the floor to find.

One woman, Mountain Mouse she was called, was the queen of the pits. She had walked the ladder so many times that on flat ground she stepped high as if she was climbing the rungs. Nick once told me that he had seen Mountain Mouse take thirteen men to the loft, drink all their whiskey, and handle a rooster in the pits the same night.

If fights broke out, and they always did, the man knocked cold was dragged to the side of the barn and allowed to bleed. I watched him closely as he rolled on the floor in pain. There was a chance he might lose some money from his pocket. But if he had made a trip to the loft earlier there would be no use to watch; Mountain Mouse had hands that moved quicker than the spurs of a rooster.

Another man as permanent at the barn as the joist that held it up was Cardinspades Mangler. He was a little man, about as tall as a gooseneck hoe and as broad across the shoulder as a sack of Middling. He seldom shaved and his beard was the same color as his white hair. He was not a Kentucky man (Lord help him) but had come to Bloody Front before the timber had disappeared from the Big Sandy, which made him an old man there as far as seniority was concerned.

"How was it you left West Virginia to come to Bloody Front, Cardinspades?" he was asked once.

"Wife sent me to buy a loaf of bread."

"Why didn't you buy the bread in West Virginia?"

"Two cents cheaper on the Kentucky side of the river."

"Two cents ain't much money."

"Enough to get a card game going here on Bloody Front. Hellhole of the world. Never got back across the river."

"Ever hear from any of your people over there?"

"Once I did. Got a letter from the wife the same year I left. 'Last chance,' she says to me. 'Come back now. Choose between me and Bloody Front.' "

"Did you choose?"

"Ain't seen her since. Poor woman."

He had spent more time in the city jail than any five police judges had remained in office. His quarters were on the same floor as the judge's—the second. The only difference was that you turned to the left at the top of the stairs instead of the right.

His greatest advantage was his ability to make friends. Cardinspades was never known to cause trouble. He was too small to fight, so he agreed with all comers. However, whenever he got drunk it was necessary to bring him to the city jail. After drinking he wanted plenty of air. He found it walking up and down the center of the streets in town. If a car had hit him, he would have had to be buried by the county.

He now held the distinction of being the only man in town allowed to sleep regularly in the women's jail. Bars still remained around his room but the big steel door was seldom locked. He came and went of the day and night as he pleased. Women were locked up inside two smaller cells in the big room.

Wherever the crowds gathered, Cardinspades could start a game of casino. On Sundays when they came over to the riverbanks for baptizing, he mingled among them, sure that someone would agree to a game of casino. At the chicken fights, the crowds were made to order for him. He hustled around the pits dragging drunks into the corners and taking a few pennies from each. He picked them as slick as I could pick a chicken—just as clean.

iii

Melvin Hickey owned a black rooster, about the biggest bird ever to fight at the barn. He was so black that the overhead lights glistened from his feathers. For many people, it had been a costly experience to learn about this rooster. One look at him would have told you why. He seemed to be nothing but a big black cull, awkward, with his feathers broken and uneven. He was one-eyed, and around this part of the country he was known as One-Eyed Blackjack, or just Blackjack for short.

Local men knew him too well, so to match him with a local rooster was out of the question. To fight, he had to wait until some drifter from out of state came here to the valley. Most of the time several men came together, bringing with them enough roosters to last the weekend. Perhaps they thought that here was a small fight outside a country town, poor breed of chickens, and men proud enough to bet heavy. The outsiders brought money to back their faith.

Melvin Hickey set up at nights waiting for this sort of men. First he matched them with bad roosters. He let them win, betting small amounts on each fight. After his bird had got the gaff, he'd shake his head and say, "You boys sure brought roosters with you. You're skinnin' me for good."

Finally Melvin would shake his head and talk as if he was in a fit of rage. "Guess that does it," he'd say. "Got nothin' left to match you with. Wait! By God, I ain't givin' up. Got one chicken left . . . if you can call him a chicken. He ain't much to look at, but he'll fight or I'll wring his neck. Damned rooster's next thing to a pet."

He'd walk out of the barn and come back carrying old Blackjack. "You boys are chicken men! You can't expect me to bet this rooster even with yours. Not with his one eye."

"What kind of odds?" the outsiders would say, sizing up the rooster, sure that all Melvin Hickey owned would soon be in their pockets.

"Well, it's all or nothing with me. If you win I'm out of the chicken business." He'd take another drink from the bottle and weave as if he were high in the wind. Little did they know that whiskey was like water to Melvin Hickey. "Make the odds right with me, and I'll put up everything I have left, even the barn itself!"

The bets were placed, and into the pit the two chickens went. Old One-Eyed Blackjack would strut before the crowd, favoring his good eye. Into the air he'd go as if Melvin Hickey was pumping air up his rear with a hose. Then you could hear the gaffs hit from any place in the barn, and the fight was over and Blackjack had another win.

Soon the one-eyed rooster was known wherever chickens were fought. Now, instead of matching the rooster, game chicken men plotted to learn what his breeding was. They never found out, and after seventeen wins the old black rooster was retired.

iv

When I opened my books at school game chickens ran along the pages. My studies faltered. I would have given all the books in the valley for just one game rooster. I dreamed high: I wanted a rooster that surpassed even Old Blackjack.

The following summer I got my rooster. If you had chosen among a thousand chickens, you could have never picked one that looked less like a champion. At the time, Nick and I were working in Melvin Hickey's barn. Chickens set along the slopes of the hills, hens hovering their brood. Occasionally a small biddie would shoot out from under a hen's wing and the rains came so hard that they beat the biddie to death before it could reach cover. Old hens would hover the dead as well as the living, believing that even in death the chick needed the warmth of a mother's wing.

I had turned to go inside the barn when I saw the small chicken keeping close to the barn to shield himself from the rain. He was a sorry-looking sight: too small for a stag and big enough to have been chased from the wings of his mother. Feathers were gone from his head and sides. But he was my rooster. I knew it. Not that I actually thought he had the makings of a fighter. Chances were he hadn't. But I had learned to favor anything handicapped—whatever seemed to have no chances. This way every step was progress.

Running loose, these hill chickens had faced a much more hazardous test than any pit. The challengers were snows, rains, snakes, foxes, hawks, and even hunters who took home a chicken instead of a rabbit. Of the winter, they milled around the barn scratching in the hay that Melvin Hickey spread out for his cattle to eat. Of the fall, they crossed the road and pecked in the corn fields for grains of corn the shuckers had accidentally knocked from the yellow ears of feed corn.

These chickens were not considered fighters. The chance that the hills would produce the perfect mixture of game blood was as rare as catching a spoonbill sturgeon in the Big Sandy River. And so the chickens hatched along the hills would run with a touch of steel. Yet Melvin Hickey was not a man to give anything away. When I told him I wanted the small chicken, he said, "Don't matter how droopy the chicken is, he'll sell as a fryer. It'll take a day's work to pay for his weight."

I did a day's work, and then I took the small chicken home and turned him out in the lot with the culls.

"Where on earth did you get this poor chicken?" Mom asked.

"Found him in the hills," I answered. "He was drowning." The sadness of a small chicken dying in the hills assured him of a home, as far as Mom was concerned.

He feathered and turned out speckled all over like a Dominicker. One black streak covered his neck and shoulders. Mom was not easily convinced the day after Nick came to trim his comb and spurs. But she was sympathetic when we told her that his comb had been frozen when he was living in the hills, and would all drop off if it were not cut. Mom knew nothing of game chickens, except that it was a mortal sin to fight them. I did not have him trimmed because I really intended to fight him. After all, this rooster had already won a thousand fights in my dreams, with Nick "handling" him all the way. Nick was lucky too. He had not had to suck blood from him even once; another rooster never got that big a jump on him. Of the evenings, I sat near the chicken lot watching the rooster go high into the air. He made his kill each time, a clean one too. That he came down on top of a hen made no difference to me. I scratched this portion from the dream.

"Let's put that rooster in condition," Guy Sparkman said to me one evening as he passed by the house. "He looks good enough to fight. Got a lot of Dom in him. That black across his back and shoulders is War Horse."

Guy Sparkman was a patrolman on the police force, a much better game chicken man than a policeman.

"I don't intend to fight him," I answered, a lump coming to my throat just thinking of it.

Guy Sparkman went into a long lecture. A squirrel was born and bred to climb a tree, dogs to bark, fish to swim, and game roosters to fight. It was in the blood of a game chicken. He must fight.

In the days that followed, we learned many things about the rooster. He was a low squatter. The jagger gaff would be fitting for him. He was slow, a disadvantage. But perhaps in his case his power would make up for the slowness. Guy Sparkman had never before seen a rooster that could knock another chicken on his rump with boxing gloves on—not even Blackjack.

When I put him in the pit for the first time, I was sure of only one thing: this was one rooster that would never be picked. I would bury him first along the slopes where he had been hatched and raised.

But there was no hole to be dug this time. His challenger went high into the air, suspended, and waited for my rooster to come up after him. But my rooster wouldn't fight that way. He squatted low to the sawdust, and struck with enough power to explode feathers into the air. One blow and it was over.

I carried him home that night as tenderly as I would have carried a hatching egg. Lucky? That's what they had said around the pit. But didn't I know better!

He fought again two weeks later. This time Guy Sparkman got a little better odds and had a little more faith. I didn't bet because I had nothing. But I wouldn't have bet anyhow. I was superstitious; if I bet, he might lose. It was a sin to fight chickens and a sin to gamble, Mom said. With two sins against me I would shorten the chances of my rooster. This fight lasted one blow, too!

He got a taste of steel in the third fight. He was knocked

on his side, and he would have lost except for a mistake by the other rooster. The rooster came shuffling in, pecking the sawdust and turning his head from side to side. My bird struck from his side and ended the fight in one blow. But he had been cut deep and so we put him "on the walk," that is, turned him loose in the hills above Guy Sparkman's house to allow him to heal.

His rest was short. He had built a reputation and he was expected to defend it. Also he had disgraced too many well-bred roosters.

He had no form, but his intelligence was something to watch. He seemed to know each move the other roosters would make before they made it. If they went high into the air, he waited and caught them off balance in the split second they were on their feet again, often maneuvering to the back of the chicken that came down. If they squatted he pretended to walk away and when they came for him he turned to nail them. He had everything but the looks of a champion.

After twelve wins, talk around the pit changed. They spoke of how they would like to have seen him matched against Blackjack. After seventeen wins none doubted my rooster's ability.

Winter came and a strange thing happened. Since the day I had brought him home, he had chosen the oaks as his resting place. This too was part of his breeding. Chickens of the hills had learned to use the high limbs of the trees for protection. He would roost no other place.

This winter the weather dropped to below zero. Morning came and the toes of my rooster turned white. Two days later they dropped off at the first joint.

"Toes gone would mean sure death for most roosters," Guy Sparkman said. "But this rooster is a squatter. Tell you what: one more fight. Fight him and I'll give you three of the best Warhorse hens I have to get you a setting of eggs from him."

What Guy Sparkman did not say was that the last fight would be in the "battle royal." The battle royal was held once a year at the pits. Five roosters were placed in the pit at the same time, with no handlers. To couple with another chicken meant death. The rooster left alive was the winner.

Into the pit went five roosters. But my bird did not run into the center of the ring to meet another rooster. He stood at the side of the pit watching like a spectator. A rooster went down, bleeding bad. A handler could have saved him, but now he strangled on his own blood. Two coupled and the fourth rooster killed them both. He turned to crow; but his crow ended in a death rattle. My stub-toed rooster had won. And he earned a name that remains here today wherever game chicken men gather: Stub-Toe the Champion.

I took him back home. I was afraid to bring the Warhorse hens to the house, so Guy Sparkman allowed me to pen the rooster with them at his place. Each day I went to the pen to look for eggs. Stub-Toe was old and he had had a lot of steel in him. Each day he lost weight. And still no eggs! Guy Sparkman had lied to me; the hens were pullets, too young to lay. One morning the champion lay on his side inside the pen. I carried him to the hills and buried him, placing a flat rock over his grave so that the foxes could not dig him up.

The steam boat "H.M. Stafford" on the Big Sandy River.

Coming down the valley by boat.

CHAPTER 13

You won't find the names of Jim Hewlett, Richard Clark, and Mason Clark listed on the roster of the Rotary Club, Lions Club, American Legion, Elks, Chamber of Commerce, or any of the other clubs in Catlettsburg. Nor will you find them listed as graduates of any of the local schools. Grandpa Hewlett and Grandpa Clark had no schooling. The school where Dad attended the first grade has long turned to dust. You wouldn't know of them at all unless you were among their own people—men and women of the hills. Here if you were to mention their names, stories of legendary proportion would sprout up around you. Grandpa Hewlett for his great strength; Grandpa Clark for his knowledge of coal and water; Mason Clark for the skill of his hands and the size of his heart.

You would be told that Grandpa Hewlett was judged by many to be the strongest man to ever roam the Big Sandy country. They would tell you of his match against two black men, Ben and John Coopen to prove it.

Ben and John Coopen were known for their strength up and down the Big Sandy Valley as far as the Chesapeake and Ohio Railroad Line ran. From the railroad tracks their reputation spread like a swollen river, deep into the hills.

They lived in a log cabin more than five miles up the valley from the mouth of the river. How many there were I don't rightly know. But since the day the first rail had been laid, there had been at least three of them working with the section gangs. Whenever one became old enough to retire, a younger man took his place. Each of them had the back of a mule and the strength of an ox. Over the years, they had become as much a part of the railroad as the long tee rails that wound through the mountains, drawing the hot sun and throwing it back against the barren hills in long silver streaks.

Among the hill people, their strength was talked about more than the railroad itself. Any of them could bend down, scoot his hands under the end of a tee rail, and lift it to his waist; two of them could pick up the ends and carry it away. No white man had ever been able to lift the end of a section of rail.

The story of Grandpa Hewlett's strength was also traveling the length and width of the valley. Unwilling to admit defeat at the hands of the black men, whites talked of Grandpa Hewlett's power to lift the great logs across his broad shoulders and carry them single-handed to the sawyer. According to legend, he had lifted and dragged logs that a mule had balked at pulling. Wherever men gathered, the strength of Grandpa Hewlett was talk-matched against the strength of the Coopen's. But it remained only talk. There was little chance that the stronger would ever be known. Railroad men and timber men did not mix. But for many years, talk of such a match had drifted along the hills as steady as a summer wind.

Then one day, for no apparent reason, Grandpa Hewlett pulled his boat to shore a few miles from the mouth of the river, and crossed the river bottoms to where a section gang worked under the hot sun, gouging out broken crossties and replacing them. New sections of rails glistened in the hot sun beside the tracks, waiting to replace the old ones.

Grandpa Hewlett walked up to the section foreman.

"Is this what you call a section of rail?" he asked, pointing to the long strips of iron beside the track.

"Reckon it is," the foreman said.

Men stopped work along the tracks to stare at Grandpa Hewlett. All of them, including Ben and John Coopen, knew Grandpa Hewlett. Men of the hills might start work before daybreak and quit after sundown, but once the job was done, they searched for pleasure. They had found it in the sweet music of Grandpa Hewlett's fiddle. Not a man among them but what had danced half a night to it. Even the Coopen's, standing under the hot sun stripped to the waist, their bronze muscular bodies pouring sweat that coated the skin with a bright finish like wax, knew him well. His fiddle music had been free to all. He did not draw a line when it came to a man's color. In fact, he had once said to Dad, "There's more music in a black man's toe than there is in the whole body of a white man." The music of Grandpa Hewlett's fiddle had seeped more than once from the cracks in the walls of the small Holy Roller church where blacks worshiped.

Grandpa Hewlett stripped to his waist. He had come to challenge the strength of the Coopen black men. He straddled the tee rail, spread out his arms and lifted them high into the air, bent over, cupped his hands under the end of the section and lifted it to his knees before he dropped it.

"More weight to steel than there is to wood," Ben Coopen, the biggest and oldest of the Coopen's, said.

Grandpa Hewlett wiped the sweat from his face. He

went through his motion again. The rail came above his knees and then passed his waist. He held it there, looked off across the hills and wrinkled his face, sucked in a breath of air and pushed the tee rail to his shoulders. There it stayed a moment, his legs trembling beneath him. Then he slid out from under it and the black dust rose as the heavy rail banged back to the ground.

Ben Coopen straddled the rail. He pulled it to his waist, sucked in a breath of air, and grinned. Spreading his legs he heaved. And as quick as a cat he was out from under the rail. The black dust rose into the air. He grabbed the rail again; but this time it went no farther. Sweat poured from his body so heavy that it soaked the black cinders beneath him. The tee rail wouldn't come higher than his waist. Breathing hard, he said to Grandpa Hewlett, "Beat us in singles, Jim. Now git you a white man and beat us in doubles. One of you on one end of the rail and one on the other!"

Grandpa Hewlett stared at each man there. Seeing the whites lower their heads to dodge his glance, he walked to the center of the rail. With a shovel he cupped out a hole under the center of it. He lowered his huge body, locked his hands together under the section. The rail tilted and then steadied. And he carried it for more than six feet.

"Knew you to be good at saw logs, Jim," Ben Coopen said. "Knew you was good at fiddling. Never thought you'd be good at tee rails. You beat us fair and square. I'm glad it was you, Jim. Boys might not have took a licking from another white man."

And Grandpa Hewlett shook hands with them all. "If I ever lift another rail, Ben, I hope you're on the other end of it." And he turned to cross the bottom back to the river.

"Just a minute, Hewlett," the foreman said. "If you'd picked a white man to lift with you who'd you have picked?"

"Had one picked if I needed him," Grandpa Hewlett said.

"Who?" the foreman asked.

"Charles Coopen," Grandpa Hewlett said, laughing as he stared at the youngest of the three black men.

"Ben said to pick a white man," the foreman said.

Grandpa Hewlett laughed so loud as he crossed the bottom that he could be heard all the way to the river. He stepped into the joeboat and paddled toward Catlettsburg.

ii

Mention Richard Clark and you might be told as I was one day by Jephy Hensley who was ninety-seven years old and a few days away from the grave when he said to me, "Never seen a man look so tall and awkward sliding through the mouth of a belly mine as Richard Clark. He humped up like a bullfrog, diggin' and stretchin' and pullin' away more coal from the walls than any three men. Best on coal and water than any man to ever traipse these hills."

Grandpa Clark had often been kidded about never seeing the sun come up or go down. Still he knew the land around him as no other man knew it. He could uncover a seam of coal, tell you the number of it, and judge how deep and thick it sliced into the earth. Would there be enough coal to labor at opening a mine here? Would the earth above the coal hold if the mine was dug? Grandpa Clark set about making his decision, realizing that the very life of a little community that had sprung up around the strike depended on his judgment.

But even more important to the people than coal was water. From water grew Grandpa Clark's reputation, a reputation that flowed deep in the backwoods as freely as the water he found.

Traveling the hills with a willow fork, Grandpa Clark searched for water. He did not prove himself in the low lands where any man that cared to dig to the river's level could strike it. He found it along the points where the clouds seemed so close to earth you could have stretched and poked a hole through them. Water that he found deep beneath the crust of earth remained cool even on the hottest day of the summers. And each cool glass to parched lips spread farther the legend of Grandpa Clark.

iii

The legend of Mason Clark was the skill of his hands and the size of his heart. Dad had begun very early to use the skill of his hands to make his living. He had crawled inside the belly mines so early of the mornings that darkness was still among the hills. Lying on his stomach and back, he picked at the black seams of coal with a small miner's pick until he had chipped enough coal to fill a burlap sack, and then he wriggled out of the mine backward, pulling the sack with him. And when he left the mine at the end of the day darkness was again among the hills. Later he had traveled the slopes, ridges, and hollows cutting the black oak, poplar, walnut, and hickory, and dragging them across the valley to the Big Sandy River where he rafted them and rode them down the currents to the river mouth.

Then one day, because of lack of money, he made himself a pair of shoes to keep out the snows. As surely as if the Lord had spoken to him, he knew that this was the skill for which his hands were intended.

Before the great flood, Dad had operated his small shoe shop in Catlettsburg. Tanning the hides himself, he took his needles and made shoes to match the skill of machinery. Later he had a shop in the basement of our house.

It was winter and the dark clouds hung over the hills as black as the wings of a crow. Then, as if the long, naked fingers of the black oaks on the ridge had stretched to puncture them, snow came and turned the valley and hills white. Late in the evening a tall, lean man walked into the shop and said to Dad, "You Mason Clark?"

"Yes," Dad answered, looking up from the piece of leather he was trimming with a shoe knife.

"Name's Tom Marson." The big man stretched out his hand. And the snow melted from his hair, exposing the blackness and the streaks of white that a man can't shake from his hair as he does snow. "Can you make a shoe?"

"Yes," Dad said, shaking his head, "I can make a pair."

"I can buy a pair at any store," the man said. "That's

the reason I came here. I don't need but one shoe."

"One shoe?" Dad asked, looking up again from the strip of leather. "If you have only one shoe made, it will outlive the other one you wear. You'll be no better off. Better have a pair made."

Tom Marson frowned and said, "Can you make me a shoe or can't you? I've walked more than twenty miles down river in snow because I was told you could. That's a long ways to walk, Mason Clark, for a missaying."

Dad placed the piece of leather on the floor and straightened up. But he straightened slow, for Dad was an old man and his hair was white as the blossoms of the locust and his skin was wrinkled as the timber-stripped hills.

"All right, what size do you wear?" he asked, squinting toward Tom Marson's feet. "Maybe I better take a measurement. A lot of work goes into the making of a good shoe. Too much work for a man to guess at the size."

"But there'd be no use for you to measure my shoe," Tom Marson said. "The shoe ain't for me. It is for my boy, Ely."

"Then you should have brought me a measurement."

Tom Marson frowned again. "I've done better. I brought the shoe itself." He pulled a worn shoe from his back pocket and handed it to Dad.

Dad looked the shoe over, turning it from side to side. Finally he said, "Well, I can make the shoe. But I can't guarantee the best work without seeing the boy's feet."

"There's only one foot," Tom Marson said, biting his lower lip. "The other is a club. He was marked with a club foot before he was born. Man can't buy one shoe at a store, and they don't make a shoe for a club. I have to buy two and throw one away."

And as Dad fingered the worn shoe he found out more about Tom's son, Ely. The boy's one shoe had had a lot of wear. But on the club foot there had never been a shoe; instead, cloth rags were wrapped around the stub and tied upon his leg with a string. The boy could hobble with the aid of a crutch and when snow was in the valley his leg was bent at the knee and tied to his leg so that the stub would not touch the snow.

"Would tomorrow be soon enough?" Dad asked. "I can make it tonight."

"I'm obliged. I'll come for it first thing in the morning." Tom stretched out his hand again. "I'm surely obliged." He turned for the door.

"Just a minute, Tom Marson," Dad said. "You won't be making the trip up river tonight?"

"No."

"Where will you stay tonight?" Dad asked.

Tom grinned. "Oh, here and yonder, I reckon."

"Be obliged to have you stay at my house," Dad said. "Not much room and maybe less to eat, but you're welcomed."

Tom Marson, like Dad, was not an educated man in the manner of books. But he was educated to hard living and to the ways and customs of the hill people. Something passed between him and Dad as silent as the snow. It told him that he was welcome at our house, and it told Dad that he would have been sheltered at Tom Marson's home.

That night in the small basement under our house,

Dad wove his needle in and out of the leather. Here he worked under the light from two carbide miner's lamps suspended from the ceiling. And as he worked into the night he said to Tom, "I'm making this shoe on one condition. And that is, you measure the distance around the club foot with a string and bring the string to me."

Tom Marson did. And Dad made a leather shield to cover the boy's stub foot. On the bottom of the shoe, he hardened the leather so that it would wear no faster than the one on the normal foot. When Tom Marson offered to pay the bill, Dad said to him: What do you have the most of on your place up river?"

"Chickens," Tom said.

"Bring me what you can spare next time you come to town," Dad said. "But don't carry over four."

The tale of Tom Marson's boy spread over the valley and passed beyond the Virginia border. And men came. Some had club feet like Ely's; others had one leg shorter than the other, in which case Dad built up the shoe on the short leg until it matched the height of the other. No matter what the affliction, Dad would put leather around it.

The story of how Tom had paid spread too. Most of the time we went hungry. But to make sure we didn't starve, Mom kept taking in washings from the neighbors, scrubbing the clothes on a board until her hands bled. Mom and Dad had learned to work together, and they ate much less than the rest of us.

There were times that, just when it seemed we would go beyond the power of suffering, the skill of Dad's hands brought food to the table. A man would walk as far as thirty miles down river, a boy strapped to his back, driving a pig in front of him or leading it with a rope. He had come to trade the pig for a special-made shoe. And Dad would tuck his collar around his neck to keep out the cold. The moon would be sifting through the trees and sprinkling streaks of light over the earth, and in this light he would walk out into the snow toward the basement, his hands in his pockets so that the wind would not stiffen them until he could not weave his needle through the leather. And wherever the soles of his own shoes touched the snow, small circles formed inside the track where the holes were. But, he would have told you, it's such a short walk to the basement. And didn't he intend to fix his own shoes when there was leather enough?

Boy with a new guitar, Shenandoah Valley, Virginia, 1935.
Music played an important role in the lives of mountain
families, like the Clarks.
Photo courtesy of Arthur Rothstein, Library of Congress (LC-
USF-33-2184-M5), Washington, D.C.

CHAPTER 14

For all of their years of playing music together, Dad at the fiddle and Mom at the piano, my parents had never been able to play for any period of time without arguing. Dad might claim that Mom had set her head to drowning out the fiddle by striking the piano like she was driving nails with a sledge hammer. Or perhaps Dad would prop his foot on the edge of the piano bench and bear down on the bow. How he thought that Mom could bear the full blast of the fiddle in her ear remained a secret that she was never able to explain to us.

"Samhill, Bert," Dad would say, "them hymns are as slow as a rabbit running across a molasses bed. I just can't pull the bow that slow. Now, strike up 'Golden Slippers' and second me if you can."

Somewhere in the song Mom would become disgusted with Dad, the fiddle, and the world in general. Maybe it would begin when she missed the chord and Dad frowned. Maybe the pat-pat of Dad's feet had got her out of time. She set her mouth together and beat down on the notes.

"Please, Bert," Dad would say, "just let me hear the fiddle once before we finish the song. I don't know whether we're playing in C or G."

Later that night Mom would mock Dad, "C or G! What did he know about music? He wouldn't know either chord if you scratched it on paper for him. Just about like his schooling."

Dad played by ear. Mom preferred to place a sheet of music before her even if she had been playing the song by ear for a long time. Mom had taken music lessons from Elvie Thompson for over a year, and to pay for the lessons she did Elvie's washings. Each evening after the lesson she would come home carrying a basket of clothes. And as she washed them she would quarrel, "Just keeps adding to the basket and teaching me less. Sometimes I think she makes up half of what's on the music sheets. One dress of hers is like washing a sheet. She'll weigh as much as the piano." Mom might have exaggerated Elvie Thompson's weight a little. But how she ever reached the keys of the piano across her belly was a miracle.

Arguments between Mom and Dad seldom ended at the piano. After we kids had all gone to bed, we could hear Mom quarrel. The music of the fiddle drifted through the bedroom. With it came the pat-pat-pat of Dad's foot. At one time the soft music of the fiddle had put us all to sleep. But Mom soon won us over to her way of seeing it. The pat-pat became the thundering hoofs of a dozen horses. Listen to it! Pat! pat! pat! Although I loved the music of the fiddle more than about anything else, I came to despise the pat-pat. Where had the music gone? Lost in the pat-pat of Dad's confounded foot!

ii

For a number of years Dad had been a member of a three-piece band called the Mountain Melody Boys. They practiced once a week, first at the Leaning Tower and now here at our house at the foot of the hills. Chet Potter played the guitar. He was a thin, wiry man, with shallow eyes that held a mark of fright in them as if he had just seen one of Mom's spirits. Joe Faraway played the banjo. He was tall and lanky. The only fat place on him was his stomach that pushed out on his thin frame as if he'd swallowed a nail keg.

The three of them would pull up chairs to form a circle in the small living room and Jerry and I would scoot as close as we could get and listen to them for hours on end. Mom would be in another room sewing or washing.

"Look at that little Billy shuffle his feet to the music," Joe Faraway would say. He'd squint his eyes at me and pucker his mouth as if he was tasting a green persimmon. Then he'd slide his fingers over the slim neck of the banjo and strike the strings with his long fingernails as if he expected the chord to astound the very world itself. Dad would frown. He did not particularly care for the music of a banjo. To him it sounded like a chicken picking corn off the top of an empty wash tub. But here in the hills you had to have a banjo in a string band. People swore by them. "Since your feet ain't moving, Jerry," Chet would say, "run take a peek and see whereabouts your mother is. Bet you got the eyes of a hawk and feet soft as a rabbit's that'll keep her from knowing you're peeking. 'Spect you better go with him, Billy. Easy now! Here's music to cross a floor without being caught."

While we were on the other side of the room, Joe would pull a little-boy bottle from his shirt, and around the circle it would go, reverse itself, and then back into Joe's shirt again. When I was back with a good report on Mom, Chet would let me take the big guitar and pick along with the music. "Beats all I ever saw," Chet would say. "Ain't no bigger than a creek minnow and he's picking the guitar. Hand me the pick box, honey, and you run and peek for your mother."

Not only had Chet won my heart but he had also won Mom's. With her this was all-important, because if she had suspected any whiskey was in the house, he would have ended up in the dirt road outside, probably with the box around his neck, never to darken our door again. But Chet could drink until his eyes were as red as the comb of a laying hen, and Mom would never become suspicious.

"Berthy," he'd say, "I sorta look forward to hearing you play a hymn song on the pi-an-o. Ain't been feeling too well lately (the little-boy bottle had traveled around the circle so fast it would have made you dizzy to watch it) and, well, a hymn kinda perks a man up."

After more coaxing, Mom would sit down, and Jerry would stand to sing the words in a voice that sounded like a mixture between a skinned cat and a feathered screech owl:

"Jesus keep me near the cross;
There a precious fountain,
Free to all, a healing stream,
Flows from Cal'ry's mountain."

Chet would set the big guitar on the floor and lean on the neck of it. His eyes would get redder by the note, and his white hair would dribble over his face. His skin looked old and wind-tanned. He was a section worker on the railroad, the coldest job of winter and hottest of summer.

"Near the cross, a trembling soul,
Love and mercy found me;
There the bright and morning star
Sheds its beam around me."

With a voice as quivering as the wind in the oaks outside, Chet would say, "Give Berthy a little second with the fiddle, Mason."

Dad would prop his foot on the end of the piano bench and try his best to match the slow hymn. Tap! tap! tap! the other foot would go. Chet would see Mom frowning and say, "I do believe you're gettin' a mite loud with your foot, Mason. A little softer on the fiddle."

A smile would come to Mom's face, and even upside down it would have read, "You see, Mason, I told you before. Now maybe you'll believe it."

Many times Chet would be just too plain drunk to carry the guitar back home with him. So he'd leave it at our house. As he left, he'd carefully choose his steps as if he were walking on nests of eggs. Mom said, "Never saw one man under conviction so bad. Salvation is pulling at his shirt." But to Chet salvation came in the form of a little-boy bottle. If the neck had popped out just once, he would never have been able to outrun Mom, drunk as he was.

The Mountain Melody Boys traveled the length and width of the Big Sandy Valley. They played for farm socials, just plain socials, funerals, baptizings, and square dances, and they pulled crowds together for stump-jump politicians.

They often crossed the rivers into Ohio and West Virginia. At only one place did they have permanent booking: a place called the Redbud Tavern. The tavern was less than three miles from the city limits of Catlettsburg. Up river to the first bend you turned back into the hills on a road that had been carved around the town cemetery and up a steep hill. The hill had long been a testing ground for used cars. Buyers were not impressed by talk that a car had been driven by an old lady who used it to take her to church. They wanted to know if it could pull Redbud Hill.

Near the top of the hill, the Redbud Tavern was built in a pocket notched in the side of red clay. Beginning with April when the redbud trees bloomed, the top of the hill was given a red headband.

The Redbud Tavern did a "good" or a "better" business, depending on the decisions of the townspeople. Local options kept the power of the wets and drys moving up and down as often as the waters of the two rivers. But local option did not apply out at the Redbud, so on Saturday nights people walked, drove cars, rode horses, and hitched rides from the hills and from town to gather there. They would drink, dance, fight, and listen to the mountain melodies for half the night.

Dad was paid five dollars a night for his fiddle. This much Mom knew and approved of. She did not know that the five dollars was in excess of all he could drink. She was not awake early Sunday morning before daylight when Dad, Chet, and Joe came past the house. Chet would be bringing up the rear, weaving like he was being whipped. Joe would have the banjo slung over his shoulder like a squirrel rifle. And Dad wasn't in any too good shape himself.

Jerry and I made our debut at the Redbud when I was nine and he was eleven. It happened one Saturday night when Joe came by the house for Dad. He was alone. Chet was sick.

"You can't play for a square dance with a fiddle and a banjo," Dad said.

"What's wrong with Billy?" Joe asked. "He picks that box about as good as Chet."

"Well. . ." said Dad, "Bert might not approve of it."

"If Billy goes I go too," Jerry said.

There was no doubt Mom was influenced by the fact that I was apt to be paid for the night's performance. "Billy is awful little to carry that big box all the way out there."

But with Jerry going along to help, we started toward the Redbud. I carried the guitar until my arms ached, unwilling to give it up to Jerry because I wanted to practice as we walked. This was a weird and beautiful place, high on a knoll with the winds sweeping across it day and night, trembling the tops of the trees and creeping down the sides of the hill to carry the scent of flowers.

The Redbud was filled with people, smoke, and whiskey. An oak platform came out from one end of the room for the band. And here, overlooking the crowd, we played music that had to fight its way through the noise and smoke. Feet went into the air both from dancing and from fights. The sawdust would soak up the blood, so the only restriction on fighting was not to fall on the dance floor.

After the first song, beer was set on the edge of the platform for Dad and Joe, and pop for me and Jerry. The man said to me, "You're playing the guitar for yours," and to Jerry, "What are you going to do for your bottle of pop?"

Jerry stopped on the pop so quick he almost choked.

"He can sing," I said.

"O.K."

"Sing the crawdad song, Jerry," I said.

"Don't push me!" he answered.

"If the little fellow can hold out the night he's entitled to half what I paid Chet," the man said.

Two dollars and fifty cents! Jerry stood up to sing:

"Yonder come a man with a sack on his back
uh huh
Yonder come a man with a sack on his back
uh huh
Yonder come a man with a sack on his back
got more crawdads'n he can pack
uh huh, uh huh, uh huh

"Asked my gal for to marry me
uh huh
Asked my gal for to marry me

uh huh
Asked my gal for to marry me
on turnip greens and blackeyed peas
uh huh, uh huh, uh huh

"Asked her again for to marry me
uh huh
Asked her again for to marry me
uh huh
She took one look'n saw my sack
like two crawdads we went back'n back
uh huh, uh huh, uh huh."

We played here for two years—Dad, Chet, and Joe making feet light and me keeping the local pop dealer in business. Jerry got himself a job with the slop dealer outside of town, but I remained with the band, traveling the length and width of the valley. One night, miles up river at Prestonsburg, I knew I was a permanent part of the band: I was asked to sign my autograph. I scribbled it across the paper, omitted the ie in "Billie" and sat back with the rest of the men on the platform.

Billy C. Clark working his trap line.
Photo courtesy of Billy C. Clark.

"I was in the third grade when I set up my first trap line."

CHAPTER 15

I was in the third grade when I set up my first trap line along the banks of Catlettscreek. The line was four miles long, two miles up creek and two miles down. By the time I reached the seventh grade, the line had been expanded to seven miles up and seven down. During those four years, I had learned many things about the country in which I lived. And the muskrat, mink, weasel, skunk, fox, and opposum furnished me with money to remain in school and to help out at home.

How well I'd come to know Catlettscreek! If the teacher had said, "Billy, on your test today at school suppose you skip the schoolbook material and write down what you know of the creek and the animals that live there," I could have told her plenty . . .

The fourteen miles each morning before class, over snags, drifts, rocks, logs, and mud, was a long distance to walk. It left me no time to skin out my catch and be in my seat when school began. I would climb the trees along the banks of the stream and wedge my catch in the forks of limbs. High up, the winter wind would keep the meat from spoiling until I could return of the evenings and skin them out. The dried leaves that I tucked around them would resemble an old squirrel's nest and keep people from robbing me of my catch.

I could never afford a pair of rubber boots, so I was forced to wade the cold winter water in low-cut shoes. I walked the creek until my feet became so numb that I no longer knew whether they touched the bottom of the creek. I stopped along the banks to break dried horseweed stalks that would burn like powder, and held my feet over the flames until the numbness was gone. The numbness passed and the pain came. The pain would not stop until my feet were in the cold water again. Halfway through the four-teen-mile trapline I would stop to eat. Crossing over into the cornfields, with the wind rattling the loose stalks of corn among the shocks, I searched for ears of corn. I brought the yellow field corn back to the creek and parched it over a fire and ate the black charred grains until my face was as black as they were, then washed my face in the icy creek. Grains of corn I shelled from the ears would fill my pockets and furnish my lunch at school that day.

Back down the creek I would walk high on the banks, close to the Catlettscreek Road, to pick up carcasses of skunks that had been hit and killed by cars during the night. A good skunk hide would bring from three to four dollars, depending on how white he was. But most of the skunks that had been hit by cars were mashed and had to be sold as damaged furs, bringing no more than fifty cents. Worse yet, many times the skunk juice followed me into the school room. As I crossed the room, the teacher and the class would turn up their noses like a bird dog winding quail. My wet shoes would be squeaking as loud as a wind can squeak and twist the old limb of a tree. Then the snow and ice melted from my clothes and it dripped in little puddles on the floor under my seat. Drip! drip! drip! I pretended not to hear it. I was thinking what a good weasel board the back of the history book would make.

My trapping had actually begun during our last winter at the Leaning Tower. In a brushpile at the mouth of Catlettscreek, I found two rusted traps, so weak from being long in the water that I could close the jaws on my hand without feeling a great deal of pain. I had been watching a big muskrat, brave enough to come out in the daytime and steal corn in the river bottoms. Always he disappeared into a hole he had wedged through the brushpile. It was here that I set the two traps. The following morning when I pulled the big muskrat from the traps I was as shocked as he had been. The muskrat had stepped into the traps, tangled himself in the brush below the water level, and drowned. As I stood on top of the brush, holding the dead muskrat by the tail, a man paddled up to the mouth of the creek in a joeboat. Across the back seat was a shotgun. He scudded the boat close to the brush and said, "Seen any ducks go up creek this morning?"

"No," I said, keeping a close eye on the big rat, not completely convinced that he was dead.

The rivers are choppy during the winter here, and the man pulled hard on the oar to keep the boat in balance. "Nice rat you got there," he said, pushing the oar against the brushpile. "Take it to Dr. Finch's office in the big building on the main corner and he'll give you a quarter for it."

A quarter! I carried the big rat up the banks as if he was

a pouch of gold. Then, starting up town, I held the big rat with his head down; his nose touched the pavement of the sidewalk. One arm became tired, and I switched him to the other; that too became tired, so I carried the rat in my arms like Mom carried my younger sister. Cars slowed down to stare at me and the muskrat, and women looked frightened and crossed to the other side of the street.

At the big building on the main corner of town I climbed a flight of stairs and stopped in front of two large swinging doors that led into Dr. Finch's waiting room. I nudged the doors open with my shoulder and walked inside, water still dripping from me and the muskrat. Several women sat there; one looked at me and her eyes fell on the rat. "Lord!" she screamed. "Dr. Finch! Dr. Finch!"

I never had a chance to tell her that the big muskrat was dead and couldn't hurt her. More women popped from their seats and screamed. I stood holding the muskrat to my side, legs straddled from the weight of it, like a gunfighter ready to draw.

Dr. Finch came into the room and squinted at me through a set of horn-rimmed glasses.

"You buy muskrats?" I asked.

"Lord help us!" a woman cried.

"Leave this office!" Dr. Finch said. "Leave it immediately!" Yet his eyes did not have the harshness of his words. He was staring not at me but at the enormous muskrat.

I was scared and turned to go.

"Not that way," he said, putting his big hand on my shoulder. "You might frighten someone else coming in to the office. This way." He circled me around the women and

Gunnell and Elk building, Catlettsburg.

"At the big building on the main corner of town, I climbed a flight of stairs and stopped in front of two large swinging doors that led into Dr. Finch's waiting room."

into his office, and said loud enough to be heard in the waiting room, "You can use the back way out!"

His big hand guided me into a smaller room. There he squatted beside me and took the muskrat. His hands moved swiftly over the dead rat, brushing back the fur, letting it fall into place, and watching the grains of sand drop to the floor.

"No cuts that I can see from the outside. But I must look from the inside." He looked up at me. "Next time you bring a rat in here, remember this: I don't buy muskrats unless they're skinned first! Now, this time I'll let you use that little room down the hall. Skin that muskrat quick, and be careful not to cut the hide. When you're through don't holler for me. I'll be back. You'll find a knife on the table inside the room."

He was gone. And here I stood in the smaller room down the hall. The knife was on a small table and the big muskrat had slipped to the floor. I stood waiting. The only door led out into the hall where I feared my footsteps would be heard. After a long wait he returned and stared at me through horn-rimmed glasses.

"Well!" he said. "Ain't you through yet? You afraid of that damned rat?"

"I . . . I don't know how to skin it," I stammered.

"The hell you don't." He looked at his watch. "If I skin it, you pay me. Is that clear?"

He picked up the muskrat and grabbed the knife and I began to shake all over. How could I pay him for skinning the muskrat? Fact is, right about now I didn't want it skinned. I didn't even want the muskrat. What I wanted was to get out of there fast!

"Here," he said, handing me the muskrat.

I took the muskrat and held it like a loaf of bread.

"Not that way!" he said. "You ain't going to rock it to sleep. You watch." I puckered my mouth to cry and a smile came to his face. "Watch and you'll learn. Being this is your first time I might just skin it out and pay you to boot. Now this is how you hold it . . ."

I took the big muskrat by the hind legs and stretched it apart as he circled the legs, cut to the rectum, and worked the hide down toward the nose in one piece. The hide came over the front paws and he ringed them, and as it came over the head he cut so skillfully that he skinned out the eyelids and the nose, whiskers and all. He pulled the hide fur side out.

"Not prime through and through," he said. "But not bad. Not bad."

He washed the blood from his hands, and hung the hide in a small closet beside more hides than I could count.

"Big muskrat like this one might have brought you as much as fifty cents if it were skinned out," Dr. Finch said. "But since I had to skin it I'm paying you a quarter. Not only will you become a trapper but I'll make a business man out of you. Here's the quarter; you go out this side door. And the next time the muskrat had better be skinned or I'll hang you, skinned out, in the room with the other hides."

When I reached the door, he handed me the carcass and said, "Take the rat to Speckle Tom on the shanty boat and he'll be apt to give you a bull nickel for it. If you see past the nickel tell him Dr. Finch will have a little-boy bottle about six o'clock."

With a ready market for the rats, I dug in the brushpiles along the creek until my hands were raw. I expanded my trap line, since both me and the muskrats were learning at the same time—they learning to escape my traps and me learning how they did it and taking them the next time. I learned to stretch their legs between trees and skin them. Out in the winter winds, the hide and carcass felt like the chunks of ice that floated along the edges of the creek.

"Damn you!" Dr. Finch would say to me. "Your head must be as hard as the bricks of this building. How many times do I have to tell you to use the side door. Damn you to hell! You bring two muskrats here, collect fifty cents from me, and chase away a two-dollar customer. Don't you know the difference between a side door and a waiting room?"

I looked up at Dr. Finch, his big eyes bearing down over the glasses, thinking how much better off I'd be if the two big muskrats were holding me instead of me holding them.

"I can't reach the handle on the side door," I told him—just in time to keep from being skinned over a board I thought.

"I'll be damned!" he said. "Your mind's the size of a minnow's pecker." He rubbed his chin. "Tell me, do you have any scruples against knocking lightly on the side door?"

"Any what?" I asked. For all I knew he might have been asking to skin me.

"Never mind," he said. "Could you knock lightly on the side door?"

"Yes."

"Lightly then."

As simple as this was, it still didn't work out very well. The first day I knocked he didn't hear me. I knocked all the harder and still he didn't come. A woman walked by and took me by the arm. "You're trying the wrong door. To see the doctor you must wait in the waiting room," she said.

I pulled to get away.

"There is nothing to fear," she said. "If you came this far, you must have good reason to see him. You poor thing. Your clothes are soaking wet."

I had been holding my brown paper sack away from

my wet clothes, but I forgot for a moment. The poke burst open and the hides fell out.

"Lord!" She screamed and threw her hands to her face. "It's a human scalp! Dr. Finch!"

"You know," Dr. Finch said, watching tears stream down my face, "sometimes, no matter how hard we try, things just don't work out." He patted me on the shoulder and led me through his office. "I'll keep the side door cracked for you. You won't have to knock in the future."

One morning I came to his office and the doors were locked. I waited but he didn't come, so I took the hides to the river and tied them in a willow. The following day the office was still closed.

"Well," Speckle Tom said to me as I sat on his shanty boat fishing for river chubs, "I guess old Dr. Finch has gone and done it good this time. Tried to cut a baby from the belly of a whore and she told on him."

Dr. Finch had paid me from a quarter to fifty cents a hide, shipped them off to F.C. Taylor and collected two to four dollars apiece for them.

iii

Most of the people of Catlettsburg claimed that Aram Stalker was a queer man. "Something ought to be done about him," they said. "It's the law's place to do it, too." But no man or woman in town wished to be known by Aram Stalker as the person that had brought the complaint.

In his sixties, Aram Stalker was short and muscular

and had the thickest, whitest hair of anybody in town. Here was a man that time seemed to have overlooked, or been afraid to touch. His skin was as smooth as the bark of an ironweed tree and just as tough. He lived in a small world of his own. Of the summers he walked the streets in short pants he'd made by cutting the legs from a worn pair of winter trousers. Sometimes he skipped like a small child. Women stared at him, shook their heads, and pursed their lips. Just think! The young girls of the town were forced to see an old man in his nakedness!

In the summer, the hot sun tormented the people, and the rivers did little to help, reflecting the heat from their surfaces up into the streets. And Aram Stalker was the only man in town to remain cool. Perhaps the only man to not give a damn what anyone said. Not that he would have known it if they had. He was deaf.

He had once been a great boxer. Old clippings that he had kept from West Virginia and Kentucky newspapers testified to his fame. In more than one of them Aram Stalker was quoted as saying, "I will fight any man, anywhere at anytime, give or take any amount of weight." Many of the older men of the town had been witnesses to his fights. They said that boxing injuries accounted for his deafness.

He had served time in the pen for moonshining. This seemed to me a distinction, marking him as a sort of hero. How often as I sat on the street curbs beside him I had wished that I had served time in prison so that I could walk the streets of town with tough written all over me. Trouble was, as he talked of the lonely life in the small cell behind the great iron bars, I knew that I only wanted his reputation, not to serve time in the pen to get it.

Aram Stalker and I were great friends, me wishing that I had his age and strength so that I could whip some people in town, and he wanting my youth and opportunity so that he could leave the town. I cut a pair of winter pants into shorts to be like him, and sat next to him on the street curb. He would read my lips like the pages of a book.

To earn his living, Aram Stalker drove a small Willys car and competed with the local taxi company for business. His aged car had been nicknamed the "Welding Rod" because the body had been welded together so many times. Local people seldom rode in Aram's taxi. His trade came from the people of the hills, far up the Sandy and deep into the hollows where no man but Aram Stalker had nerve enough to drive a car. His customers came each Saturday to shop in town and to wait for Aram Stalker to take them home. To keep from paying the price of a taxi license, he did not charge rates for hauling people. Just whatever you wished to give him. If the poorer country people didn't have money to pay him, that was all right, too. He would accept anything—hogs, chickens, corn, potatoes, and, of the winter, varmint hides.

He was a permanent fixture at the local drugstore, which served as his office. People came there to find him after their shopping. He was handy around the drugstore, and he even helped stock the shelves with merchandise. For assorting and shelving the magazines, he had the privilege of reading them. He read most. He was knowledgeable on all things, past and current, and could talk about anything. A man couldn't answer, and often couldn't even excuse himself, so Aram would talk for hours. Only the coming of a taxi customer could save the victim.

Aram Stalker was everything I wanted to be when I grew up. He lived as he pleased and asked no man for anything. He ate dry bread with mold on it because he said it was good for you, and he could walk all day along the creek bank without getting winded. Along the banks of the creek he recited poetry, mostly poems he himself had written while locked in the small prison cell. Nights he roomed in an old hotel known as the Shivley House. He felt sentimental about the hotel and did not mind in the least that most people considered it a dump where river trash gathered. In its heyday, the old building had held a place of honor in the town, Aram said, old and ragged as it was, it had more dignity than most people hereabouts.

In the timber days, the old hotel had been the best this side of Cincinnati, and the other side, too. The entire first floor of the building had been nothing but one big saloon, and men that were men placed their foot upon the brass foot rail that curved around the bar like a golden railroad track. Big timber men from Louisville, Cincinnati, and the likes came here, and they booked rooms at the hotel for weeks in advance. They drank, talked timber and women, made bids on both, left the timber at the river, and took the woman to their rooms.

Now that the timber was gone, the hotel grew old with neglect. The big brass foot rail was sold for junk. The building was rented to the poor, and strongly disapproved of by the Younger Women's Society. The owner bought a few gallons of paint and a little wine (depending on how

The Shivley Hotel on Center Street in Catlettsburg.

"In the timber days, the old hotel had been the best this side of Cincinnati, and the other side, too."

many winoes he needed to paint the place) spread the paint as thin as water, and the hotel was uncondemned.

Before I had graduated from the eighth grade, Aram Stalker and I had become partners on the trap line. Of the mornings, I crossed the town and walked up winding stairs to his small room in the Shivley House where he slept. The building was old and dark inside and smelled dank. I stopped along the stairs and stared into the darkness to see ghosts of an earlier day. I saw them walk in their fancy clothes and heard their laughter in the wind that swept through the cracks of the walls. Perhaps even Grandpa Hewlett had placed his foot on the big brass foot rail.

I opened the door of the small room and walked over to the old cot where Aram slept and touched his shoulder. He would grin and look up, and slide on his shoes. Then he reached to the floor and broke a chunk of moldy bread in half and we ate breakfast before going out into the wind.

In the early morning hours, he would grind the Welding Rod to start it, and the wind would be sweeping up from the rivers into the car's broken windows and I'd hover down in the front seat willing to bet anything that the car wouldn't start and we'd end up walking. I was always wrong, and we started across town to the road that followed the creek.

Aram Stalker was proud of this car and he'd turn toward me and say, "running smooth?" And I'd rear back in the seat (not too hard, though, because when I'd reared back just like this once before, the back of the seat gave way) and try to grin and shake my head like you do when you say, "best I've ever seen or heard." And he'd smile bigger than ever, and step down on the gas—but the only thing that moved were parts of the Welding Rod. Then there'd be a jump and a quiver, and the vibration of the motor would shake me like a concrete mixer. When we finally got moving, the wind would whistle past the cracks in the window as if we were traveling two hundred miles an hour.

Why did I lie to my great friend Aram Stalker and make him believe that the car was running smooth? Well, for one thing, I had made the mistake one morning of being truthful and telling him that there was an awful knock under the hood. And he stopped it right then and there and we stepped out into a cold drizzling rain. Then with me holding up the hood until my fingers became numb, he searched for over an hour without locating the reason for the noise.

But for all its failings, there was a real advantage to trapping with the Welding Rod. We didn't have to cover the entire length of the creeks now. We could spot the choice locations along a creek, make our sets, and travel on to another stream. We could cover thirty or forty miles a day. There was still another good thing about having Aram Stalker as a partner. Most of the people that lived along the streams, miles from nowhere, were his taxi customers, and they let him cross and trap their property at will.

He was a good trapper. He had trapped these same streams long before I was born, and his memory served him so well that even after long years of absence he remembered where old dens had been. Many of them had been kept open. We both waded the cold water to make sets, me on one side of the creek and him on the other, stopping long enough to correct mistakes I made. He moved along the creek as smooth as water without wind to riffle it.

Even though I knew he could not understand unless he watched my lips, I talked freely to him. The creek became lonely without anyone to talk to. Sometimes he would stop suddenly, stare at me, and say: "I heard you say something!"

He would hit his head with the butt of his hand as if he expected to knock out whatever it was that blocked his hearing, then, laughing, walk into the corn bottoms and come back with a couple of ears of corn. We would parch them over a fire and then he would pull out a heel of bread that had been thrown away back at the drugstore, and we ate.

Nearing the time of World War II, scrap iron, rags, and rubber sold for a fair price at the junk yards, so I carried a sack with me along the creeks. People used the steep banks of the streams for dumps and here at the dumps were perfect places to trap weasels. So while Aram made the sets I gathered junk. What I earned from the scrap was mine to keep; Aram would take no part of it. I made good money this way. Most of it bought books, paper, and other school supplies, plus a little extra food.

Evenings we traveled to the hills to make our fox and skunk sets. We passed caves deep in the hollows and Aram would stop long enough to show me the leavings of moonshine stills—a deep hole, a piece of copper tubing, an old barrel, a small dam blocking a stream, or the simple leavings of a fire in a cave. More than once, deep in the hills, we would come upon moonshiners and Aram would take me by the arm and lead me away. He knew too well what could happen to a stranger who made the mistake of going too close. Often of the nights, after the work was done, we would sit out under the trees and sky, and he would relive his days of running whiskey. If I mentioned I had seen moonshiners over on Front Street, he'd say, "No! You've seen bootleggers, not moonshiners!" He said he hated to speak of moonshiners in the same breath as bootleggers. The moonshiner at least worked hard for his money. He dodged three laws: local, state, and federal. The bootlegger in local option territory dodged only one, the local law. And in many places there was little need in dodging, unless you had failed to pay off local officials. "Of all the low-grade human beings on earth, bootleggers were lowest," declared Aram.

Aram Stalker had sold his whiskey for twelve dollars a jug in times when the best of it brought no more than six, proving than even in this lowly business he was an expert. To him moonshining was an art, just as true as day would follow night. He built a "groundhog still." This consisted of three wood barrels buried in the ground. Many men used steel barrels to simmer their mash, but not Aram Stalker. He believed that boiling mash in wood added an unbeatable flavor. Wood tempered the taste of whiskey just as hickory smoke tempered a ham. In his small cabin, Aram once kept a seven-gallon wooden keg attached to the bottom of a rocking chair. In this barrel the moonshine was seasoned.

Up above the still, Aram had set a fifty-gallon wooden stave barrel in the ground. Here he made his mash. He took a peck of corn in a burlap sack, dipped it in water, and laid it in the sun until it sprouted. Then he ground it up, sprouts and all, in a food chopper and put it down in the mash barrel. Next he poured a peck of chop (the kind of corn you feed chickens) into the barrel, and added scalding water and stirred. After he had stirred the corn and water for about fifteen minutes, he filled the barrel the rest of the way with cool water from the brook until the water in the barrel was blood temperature. Aram did not use commercial sugar, because this was one of the ways a moonshiner got caught. Stores were checked to see who had purchased large quantities of sugar. So along the banks of the creek, Aram grew his own sugar cane, and turned the cane into sorghum molasses. It took ten gallons of molasses for the mash barrel. After he added the molasses he stirred the barrel for about five minutes. Then, he dissolved a pound of yeast in the barrel and added a gallon of barley malt. If the weather was hot the mash would "work off," or "ferment" in from four to five days. If it was cold, it would take closer to seven. As the mash "worked" a sizzling sound came from the barrel, like a running creek. When the mash was ready, the barley malt would stop working and would fall to the bottom of the barrel. And the liquid would have a clear, green color and would taste like a half-ripe persimmon.

The liquid of the mash barrel was dipped off and poured into the number-one barrel. And the second and third barrels were partly filled with cool water. The fire was started under the number-one barrel and heaped high until the mash began to boil and then the fire was "pulled back" to prevent the still from puking. The liquid in the barrel turned into steam, with the larger percent being alcohol, and traveled out of a tube and into the second, or thumper, barrel. Here the steam bubbled through the cool water, heating this water until it also became steam. The bubbling of the water in the thumper barrel made a thumping noise and gave the number-two barrel its name. Then the steam traveled out of this barrel, into a tube that coiled through the number-three, or flake, barrel. Here the cool water condensed the steam and it became liquid again and ran out of a spout, called the "worm," as moonshine.

Aram was not a man to "double back." Doubling back meant adding more molasses, water, and barley malt to the same mash and running it again. Some moonshiners doubled back and made three runnings off of one barrel of mash. But this was cheap whiskey, and little more than water. They would run whiskey through the still until they could catch a cup from the worm and toss it into the fire and it would not flash.

A fifty-gallon barrel of mash made from ten to twelve gallons of good whiskey. At first these twelve gallons had been enough. But business was good. Another fifty-gallon barrel was added. And then another, and Aram took on partners. One night he and two of his partners were sitting in a car along the hollow road not too far from the still. A car drove up, a man got out and asked "What have you got in your car?"

"Why don't you look for yourself?" one of the three said.

He did. But his head was blown off in the process, right off to his shoulders. Who fired the shot? No one ever knew. Aram Stalker avoided being convicted for murder, but he was sent to the pen for moonshining. Greediness had got him in the end, so he said.

Living in the past was Aram Stalker's only mistake in our years of trapping together. To him muskrat was small game; money was in mink. But mink had become scarce here in the valley, while muskrat was still quite plentiful. The trap set for a mink might easily stay the winter without being touched. Aram Stalker could not see the changes that were taking place in the country around him. Houses had sprung up around the banks of the streams and hard-topped roads replaced the tram roads. Mink did not choose to stay close to civilization. Muskrat were not so particular.

During our last winter together, Aram walked the banks of the creek setting only for mink, and catching none. One morning he stopped me and pointed at the tip of a sandbar in the stream and cried, "Look!" A big mink had swum to the tip of the bar, he said. Actually it was not the track of a mink—only a house cat that had come during the night to search for bank rats. "He'll come back down the creek," Aram said. "and he won't vary an inch from the path he went up." He made two sets here. Two traps lost to a house cat!

Minks often traveled muskrat trails, while muskrats seldom traveled the trails of minks. Sets for minks were often made high on the banks under tree roots, rock cliffs, and hollow logs. But the muskrats stayed near the stream. Many of the mink sets were bait sets: a redbird or a field mouse. Aram would tie the leg of a field mouse with a string and stake him behind a trap. The screams that he made to gain his freedom would draw the mink. And the screams followed me long after we had left the creek. I hated field mice, but I would not make them suffer this way. I preferred sets without bait.

Finally Aram gave up trapping completely, since he had the Welding Rod to make money. When winter came again, I knew that I would walk Catlettscreek alone to set my traps. I might take few mink, but the redbird that quarreled at me in the low branches of the willows early of the mornings would have no reason to fear me. The checks for the muskrats would come again from Sears's raw fur market in Chicago or Memphis. They would pay for my schooling and help out a little at home.

CHAPTER 16

The day I swam the great Ohio River I thought that I was just about the biggest hero in town. Of course there was no band, no crowd to greet me when my toes touched the soft sand bottom of the Ohio shore. I slipped across the streets of town one summer day just before I was promoted to the fifth grade and swam the river alone.

There were few boys in my class who could do more than dog-paddle. Most of them had been taught to fear the rivers. The rivers were demons that could sneak up the banks and leave you homeless. Because most boys were afraid, the two rivers hid their beauty from them. Rivers, like people, had their moods. Neither man nor river was pleasant when their mood was bad.

Few cared that money could be made along the banks of the rivers, but I did. A person who is hungry will search for all sorts of ways to make money. Then, too, I thought that money alone would make me equal to my classmates. After all, this seemed to be the only difference among us. In Catlettsburg you were either well-to-do or you were as poor as a whippoorwill. You were judged by the clothes you wore, the house where you lived, the supplies you brought to school.

From where or how the money came seemed to matter very little. The bootlegger on Front Street was an example. He was respected; said to have more money than he could burn. Like timber and paddlewheel boats in the old days,

Shanty boat dry-docked on the Kentucky side of the Ohio River.
Photo courtesy of Billy C. Clark.

"I could peddle the bottles at Speckled Tom's shanty boat, or if he was full up, along Front Street."

the sign of wealth was the important thing.

I had begun to make money along the rivers at the age of six. I sat along the sand, a string tied to a willow pole, a red worm on a bent safety pin at the end of the string. During the month of May, the small shiners were in the rivers. I caught these minnows and sold them to fishermen. The minnows brought only a bull nickel for a hundred, but the rivers were full of them and they sold quicker than you could jerk them out. A fisherman with a trotline needed all he could get.

Later, I traded the willow pole for the gooseneck hoe, working the narrow strips of corn land on the Kentucky side until my back became so sore that I could hardly bend it, and I made twenty cents a day. I did not earn this every day, because sometimes I would be blinded by the hot sun and cut a corn sprout instead of a weed, or I would stagger under the sun and tramp down a young sprout. Either way the small corn shoot cost me a penny of my earnings. And there was no chance to cheat here in the corn field. Once a shoot of corn was cut or broken there was no power on earth that could bring it back to life. Stick it back into the ground and the sun would burn it; sneak it from the field, and the hill where it had belonged would stick out like a sore thumb. I tried both.

Of the summer, after a day in the fields, I turned back to the rivers. Summer was the time to find frogs, turtles, fish, and little-boy bottles. I peddled the frogs, turtles, and fish on the main street of town. I could peddle the bottles at Speckle Tom's shanty boat, or if he was full up, along Front Street.

The summer days along the rivers began early for me. I crossed the streets of town before the fog had lifted from the surface of the rivers. Fog quilted the town, sifting through the openings of buildings like thin clouds trying to rise and make it back above the ridges where they belonged. I carried a bucket of bait with me, crawdads and minnows. At the river I would change their water and bait them live on the hooks of my trotlines. If I was lucky, I carried a loaf of bread.

At the mouth of Catlettscreek, I set the bucket down and stretched and listened to the currents of the river play with snags and the drifting joeboat I had tied here.

Higher on the bank, still hidden by fog, were the remains of an old willow tree. It had been beaten by the rivers and most of it had long ago gone down the currents. The huge stump had tried to sprout again but her limbs had made no height, and the stump set now like the brown body of a daddy long legs, the long slender branches stretching out for legs. On top of the stump I had extra nibs for my trotline and inside the green legs I hid the joeboat oars.

Since the sixth grade, I had kept two trotlines in the rivers. The first line was just below the mouth of the Big Sandy. It was tied to a willow on the Kentucky shore, bowed to miss the sandbar at the mouth, and anchored just off the West Virginia point. Here where the two rivers met, their shouldering made a backlash and fish came from both rivers to eat food caught there. My trotline was not passed by any fish that came out of the big Ohio to feed in the

Lock No. 1 of needle dam on the Big Sandy River, Catlettsburg.

"The first line was just below the mouth of the Big Sandy." (Author's note: Where I worked lifting needles during high water, and my favorite catfish hole.)

Bridge crossing the Big Sandy River at Catlettsburg.

"Up the river early of the mornings I pulled in at the snag that held my trot..." (Author's note: The bridge that spanned the river furnished a beacon during fog for the location of my second trot.)

smaller stream.

The currents took bait from the hooks as well as bringing fish. It was a never-ending job to keep the big trot baited. This required scuddling a joeboat to the line and pulling the line over your legs, using it to steady the boat, while you slipped on bait and dodged hooks likely to pierce your legs. The nib lines were three feet long to allow them room to dance with the undercurrent and attract fish. Their length also meant that they snagged water-soaked logs and debris.

Up the river early of the mornings I pulled in at the snag that held the trot, dipped my arm up to my shoulders into the water, and fingered for the line. The long trot hummed from the currents. Holding my breath I hoped for a jerk. The small tugs at the line meant fish somewhere on the nibs and a good fisherman could tell just from the pull how large and how far out. With luck the nibs would hold only catfish. A catfish would live long out of the water, and if I did not take enough on the first raise to sell, I could hold them over for two or three raises. When I felt a jerk I went directly out the line to take the fish before he worked free of the hook. If I felt only the current I went slower, baiting on the way out.

Slowly now I nosed the boat toward the Kentucky shore line and into the Big Sandy. I checked the turtle sets I had made along the edges of the banks, on snags and low-hanging willows. Daylight came gradually.

A river is a beautiful place at morning. As daylight sprinkles through the trees the world is quiet, as if holding its breath afraid that daylight would pass it by and leave it again in darkness. The fog thins and trails off leaving the blue surface of the river underneath it. The water becomes as green as the leaves of the willow, sycamore, maple, and water birch along its banks. The hum of the current breaks the silence as it plays with snags, mud bars, and bends in the river. Daylight, and the river world is alive. The gray catbird spots the joeboat and follows it, quarreling, hoping to lead you from her nest. The kingfisher swings into the air and circles the river for his breakfast. Mudhens shoot out from along the banks, spot you, and disappear under the surface to come up where you never guessed they would.

From the hills the crows appear like a dark cloud that brings rain. They caw-caw-caw, flapping their black wings and sailing to the corn bottoms along the shores. Behind the crows comes the sun and the heat of the day.

Not far from my second trotline the river bends. Downstream from the bend there is a small cove. Here I stop to rest. I am out of the current and will lose no distance on the river. Resting the oars over the gunnels of the boat I eat a couple of slices of bread, washing them down with a drink from the river. River water is filthy, I have been told; a million little germs crawl in it. But it never hurt me. The bread is good and the water fine to wash it down. I have eaten so much bread here by the river that the fishermen along the banks nickname me the Bread-Eater. For food there is also old corn from last year's shocks in unplowed bottoms. I often have a channel catfish dangling from a string over the gunnels. I could roast him. But bread is enough. I eat it and look over the river and wonder what the second trotline a mile up stream will hold.

The sun becomes hotter on my way to the second trot. The oars scream inside the dry locks. But a dip of river water on each will quiet them.

If the garfish are heavy in the rivers, I will bait with doughballs today. Garfish will not eat doughballs. I hate to bait the trotlines with doughballs because they will catch carp and buffalo but few catfish. Neither carp nor buffalo will sell well in town. People think they are dirty fish and live only around the sewers that empty into the rivers. If the carp and buffalo are dirty fish, I think, it is because people have made them that way by allowing their sewers to empty into the rivers. I also dislike carp and buffalo because they are weak fish, and die but a short time out of the water. Their flesh is so flabby that they will not hold with a stringer through their gills; the stringer will cut through, and they will be lost to the rivers.

Many of the people in town didn't know that they ate carp and buffalo on many occasions. More than once I sold both to the restaurants in town, dressed out as catfish. Some folks never knew the difference. Others bought them with an "I-won't-tell-if-you-won't" added to the low price they gave me. With both the fish and myself in low society, I had to fool someone to stay alive.

Worse than the worry of catching carp and buffalo was the thought that gars might be in the rivers. The garfish was such a useless, ugly fish. They seemed to be afraid of nothing. Often I sat on the end of the boat baiting a trot and had them follow close enough to snip the bait nib after nib the moment it reached the water. I even had them come out of the water for a minnow if I was slow in stringing it on a hook. I took the oars and struck at them and watched them turn over in the water and dive back for the bait on the nib lines. If I stunned one with the oar I grabbed him and beat him time and time again against the side of the boat. Then I would tie him somewhere along the trotline. Old fishermen claimed that this had the same effect as a scarecrow in a corn field; it would scare other gars away. But I have seen crows build nests in scarecrows and I have had my line stripped with dead gars strung every twenty feet along it.

My second trotline was at the mouth of Chadwickscreek, a small mountain creek that wound its way for many miles through rough country. Its mouth was a perfect place for a trotline. Small minnows swam in and out of the creek and at night large fish came to the shallow water to feed on them. I caught catfish up to eight and ten pounds here.

After raising and baiting this second trot, I tied the joeboat at the mouth of Chadwickscreek, gathered the fish I had taken from both lines, and walked back to town carrying them over my back on a stringer, the flies blowing both me and the fish—big green flies, the kind that pester and keep coming. I would stop in town and sell the fish for whatever people would pay for them. This was the one part of fishing I disliked. The sun would be hot and the flies would swarm around the fish, as I stood barefooted with my feet caked in river mud and my hair matted and mixed with the fuzzy white blooms of the willow. What fish I could not sell I took home to eat. They were always welcome there.

Late of the evening I walked back to Chadwickscreek

and sat down to wait until the shadows appeared on the river. With darkness would come the croak of great river frogs. When the river is quiet, their croaks seem to shake the banks. If you listen close, you can tell their location. A frog can teach you many things about the weather. If he is low to the water, the weather will be cool. If he is high on the banks the weather will be hot and humid. You can depend on it.

If the frog was slow in croaking, I cupped my hands over my mouth and mocked him. He would always answer because summer is his mating season. Knowing his location, I eased the boat from the shore and drifted down river. All I needed to take him was patience, a good flashlight, and a sack. The light would blind him and I would snatch him from the banks. Sometimes he'd be out in the water riding the top of a brushpile and I'd ease over the side of the boat and swim for him.

Other times, as I drifted down the black river, I would see beams of light from boats on the bank, and men would holler and laugh and throw their whiskey bottles into the river. I knew many of the men that frogged the rivers. Tom Stumbo used a long-handled gig to punch out the frogs' guts. If his blow was too hard he'd leave the frog on the banks. If not he'd put him in a sack and the sack would be red with frog blood before the night was over. Always a couple more men from Front Street came with Tom to butcher the frogs and drink whiskey. Jim Meadows and Alvie Burton shot frogs under the flashlight beams with rifles. They never gathered them up; just shot them and went on. Some frogs they would catch alive and when morning came they would push straws up their rears and turn them loose in the river. The big straws kept the frogs from going under, and as they swam the surface Jim Meadows and Alvie Burton shot them.

Frogs brought good money, better than fish. A medium-sized frog sold for fifteen cents, a large one for a quarter. The local men's clubs bought all that I could catch. I walked inside any of the clubs as free as a member. I cleaned the frogs in the back rooms of the clubs and the managers offered me beer, whiskey, or pop while I worked.

Beer and whiskey! Wasn't the town dry? Well, the local option law didn't apply to the clubs. Bankers, merchants, police officers, and others came here to drink and play cards! Men would be inside the clubs soaking up booze and outside their wives would be fighting for the drys in the coming election.

Church people marched on the town holding signs that read: BRING MY DADDY HOME WITH MILK INSTEAD OF WHISKEY; WINE IS A MOCKERY; GOD RULES THE WORLD; VOTE WET AND SELL YOUR SOUL. They sang hymns and prayed on the streets. But the sun was hot and men from the march sneaked into the clubs for a cold beer.

The clubs had few membership restrictions. If you were registered at the draft board, you were a veteran eligible to join the American Legion. "Overseas Veterans" were men who had crossed the Ohio River and were eligible to join the V.F.W. The dignified Elks catered to bankers and merchants. They kept their entrance restrictions strict until finances were low and then they called a meeting of the board and lowered their standards a little. What a fine thing it would have been if they had raised the price of the frogs at those meetings.

Front Street, Catlettsburg, during high water.

"In May the rivers rose, and the scare delayed the school's order for caps and gowns."

CHAPTER 17

I needed a cap and gown to graduate from the eighth grade, and both cost money. I had made enough money to pay for them, but money had been as hard to keep in my pocket as a hot cinder. Either it went for schooling or to Mom.

Mom told me that it was a great waste to pay money for the rental of the cap and gown because I wouldn't own it. But I heard her crying softly at night because I wouldn't be graduating in a cap and gown like the rest of my class.

It shamed me when my classmates spoke of their caps and gowns. Graduation day became like doomsday for me. Sorrow for myself rooted deeper still. Perhaps, I thought, others in my class wouldn't be so eager for cap and gowns if they had to pay for the rentals themselves, as I did, by working in the fields.

After graduation there would be summer vacation—and then high school! But no summer vacation for me. I would spend the long hot days in the fields of Ohio and along the rivers. And high school? I didn't dare think of it. Would I ever be able to go on to high school?

Grammar-school graduation meant a lot to me. I had never missed a day because of sickness. I was toughened to the weather of the valley. When others had been kept home because of rain, I walked to school with my head high in the air so that the rain could hit me square in the face, wetting my clothes to the skin. I had learned to love rain. There was a cleanness about it. I may have smelled in school when the drying commenced, but the hell with it.

The teacher said we were laying a foundation that could make any of us president; but this seemed unimportant to me. Who would want to be president and spend all of his time indoors? What would people say if, one morning, the president came in from his trap line holding two big muskrats in each hand, water dripping on the carpets, on his way to skin them out!

Of the evenings now, I stopped longer at the shanty boat where Speckle Tom lived. We had been friends since the first day I had visited his shanty boat. I respected his knowledge of the river and was grateful for his interest in my schooling. You would have thought he was a college professor the way he went on over education.

Actually he was just a queer-looking black man with no schooling at all. As a small boy he had been trapped in his parents' house by fire. Somehow he had crawled from the flames, but wherever the flames had licked his body they had turned the skin as white as any white man's. For the rest of his life, he had to live with skin as speckled as a rock catfish. Small children, both white and black, laughed at his odd color.

Speckle Tom bootlegged on the shanty boat. His customers were white men. When the town was dry, they came to his boat to drink. When the town was wet, they came to his place to sober up before they went home. Either was quite all right with Tom. Of the mornings, when men woke sick on his boat, they craved a shot of whiskey to take away the sickness. He competed with the bootleggers on land, and he was clever. His shanty boat drifted far enough out in the rivers to be safe from a surprise visit of the law men. It remained there like an ancient castle I had studied about at school. His drawbridge was a sun-warped oak plank reaching from the deck of the shanty to the shore.

If the lawmen wanted to come, Speckle Tom knew that the board would not stop them. So at the first warning he would lower the whiskey jugs over the side of the shanty, and the strings that held them passed for fishing lines.

On Saturday nights the shanty boat did a booming business. And on Sunday mornings I hid under the willows and watched the drunks try to make it across the plank to shore. Their faces became so familiar to me that I kept count each Sunday as to who made it and who didn't. I scratched their names in the sand. And if the wind and rain hadn't erased their names from the sand, people here in the valley would be shocked to read them today. The aristocrats became acrobats. Into the water they went, and came out as fast as a man being baptized.

I had long been selling frogs to Speckle Tom, but things got so rough on his boat that I had stopped going there at nights. Drunks had tried to force whiskey down me and once they took off my pants and told me to walk home naked. Speckle Tom had pulled a knife to get my pants back for me. "We'll kill him if we catch him with the knife closed up," they said.

ii

There was a standing joke at our house about high school.

"I went through high school," James would say, "all

265

the way through. Walked right in one door and out the other."

"I will graduate from high school," I said.

"Big-headed!" one of my sisters answered.

In May the rivers rose, and the scare delayed the school's order for caps and gowns. So, to my joy, our grammar-school class graduated without them.

CHAPTER 18

Long, hot summer days in the fields of Ohio and two more miles added to my fourteen-mile trap line that winter supported my first year of high school.

It had been a hard winter. Rains and snows soaked the earth. The rivers rose during the flood months. The same old process of moving to high land began again. Schools were closed to students, and those on higher ground were opened to flood victims. Moving people was slow this year, since many of the men who usually did this work were away fighting World War II. There was plenty of work for any boy of size.

I had little size—one hundred three pounds jammed into a stocky frame—but what I lacked in size I made up in my knowledge of the rivers and the hardness of my body. I could handle a joeboat or a skiff as well as any man in town. During the first week of the flood, I was hired by the city to handle one of the government skiffs loaned for the duration of the high water. .

There was a lot of work to be done. The rivers had come fast, leaving many families surrounded by water. The town would have to move them. They would be hauled to high ground in the white skiffs. My job was to handle the oars in one of the skiffs.

It was customary for the city to move the people who were too poor to pay for having this done themselves—the poor in the day so all could see; the prosperous at night when the world was blind. The two rivers crested and stretched over the town pouring through the alleys and into the windows of the buildings. Back and forth I went, pulling on the big oars. People would huddle to one side of the skiff and tilt the boat until only one oar dipped deep enough into the water to take a bite. Motioning them back to the center, I would glance over my shoulder long enough to pick out a marker up ahead to guide me.

We worked days into nights and nights into days. I rowed the skiff until my back became so sore and stiff it hurt to straighten up. It was actually a relief to bend over the oars again and not have to change position. I closed my eyes when I pulled against the strong currents, as I had done many times on my way to the trotlines, and dreamed that I was somewhere else. A hollow would be a good place— deep under the shade of the trees where the quarreling birds would lull you to sleep. If I nodded, I was punched by someone in the boat.

I stayed at the oar locks until I was forced to stop and rest. I went to the third floor of the City Building and in a small concrete room I stretched out on an army cot to sleep. Over me I pulled a blanket that had more holes in it than a fish trap. Water splashed against the sides of the very building where I rested.

The Younger Women's Society had set up a kitchen on the second floor of the courtroom. They cooked meals for the city workers. Now I sat at a table afraid of dirtying the fancy table cloth. Beside my plate were two forks, a knife, and two spoons. I did not enjoy eating here. I wished that I could stand in line at school, as I often had. Stares that I got would at least be from my own people. But here I had two forks by my plate, not knowing which was for which. Each meal I waited for someone to touch a fork so that I would not choose the wrong one. Who in the hell needed two forks anyway!

After the rivers fell, people gathered to push muck and brush back off the town. So for a time I worked on for the city, washing down the streets with a fire hose, breaking mud that had dried in the wind. Again we labored into the night, and the wind blew cold sprays of water over us. Others shivered, but this water seemed warm to me. Not like the cold water along the trap line.

One evening we turned the water off and watched the rivers creep back like whipped yellow dogs within their banks. I was tired and went back to the City Building to rest. Below me, people were laughing and cursing and the smell of the muddy water was everywhere. Downstairs the kitchen was being moved out. Now the police courtroom would be needed once more to handle the drunks.

ii

I woke early the following morning and my joints and muscles ached. The smell of the rivers was worse than it had been the day before. The town was completely uncovered and the wind had grown stronger, carrying the odor. Now, for days to come, the sun would dry the films of muck, and the wind would pick it to pieces.

I looked around at the small concrete room—at the army cot and a rusty old heating stove in the center. These things kept the room from being naked. Two windows behind the cot rattled from the wind. Through them you could see back to the hills which overlooked the town. As I stared, a dream began to form, and my heart beat faster. How I wished I could live here permanently!

I remained in town the rest of the day carrying wood and helping build fires in the buildings. At the end of the day, I walked back up the three flights of stairs to the concrete room and gathered my belongings. High school would reopen within a few days now. How much longer would I be able to remain a part of it? There were complaints at home, because I woke the family when I got up so early to run the trap line or do homework for an hour or two before school. Then, too, I could study very little at nights because electricity was too expensive for the Clarks.

On the second floor of the City Building, I ran smack into a councilman. He looked at me and smiled.

"Well, Billy," he said, "got something for you." He handed me a check from the city for fifty dollars. "Not much for the work you've done."

I looked at the check, squinted my eyes, and looked again. "Thanks," I said.

"You've earned it," he answered. "Wish it could be more. Boy putting his way through high school needs it." I turned toward the hills now. It was hard to believe that the check was real.

The next morning I walked back to town. I went straight to the councilman's office, hesitated outside his door, took a deep breath, and walked inside. Avoiding his look, I told him that I would like to live on the third floor of the City Building so I could go on to high school. I expected nothing.

Catlettsburg City Building.

"...I told him that I would like to live on the third floor of the City Building so I could go on to high school. I expected nothing."

"Well," he said. "I just don't know." He looked at me and smiled. "You've got spunk! And you've proved yourself a worker as far as I'm concerned. I know the problems you face at home. Be damned! If a boy is that determined to get an education, I'll stick my neck out and let everyone in town take a whack at it! I'll recommend appointing you a member of the Volunteer Fire Department—three dollars a fire, one fifty for each drill you attend, and five dollars a month for sleeping upstairs so you can be handy for night fires."

I crossed the town again toward home, whistling. The world was a wonderful place to live in.

iii

There was little rumpus when I left home to live at the City Building. Dad showed no emotion at all. But then, it was not his way to show emotion. Mom's biggest worry seemed to be the fact that I would be sleeping three stories high from the ground. She watched me closely to see that I took everything that I would need. She seemed to have little feeling about any of us leaving since James and Bob, and now Jerry, had gone off to war.

She even seemed to talk differently now, as though I was old enough to be on my own. As she helped me gather my things, her blue-veined hands showed more than ever the years she had been struggling for all of us. I was fourteen now and old enough to be out from under her wing. She had hovered each of us while we were small. That was enough.

I walked out of the house promising Mom that I would not fall from the third-story window.

"Billy has been higher up in trees along the hills than he'll ever be on the third floor of the City Building," Dad said.

Of all that I carried with me, the steel traps and fishing cords seemed the most important. The weather was breaking and the fish would soon be running in the rivers. Winter would come and I would need the steel traps.

Even though I had slept several nights in the small concrete room, it seemed strange now. This was my new home. The room looked ugly and lonely, and the wind shook and rattled the two windows. I lit the stove, keeping the flame low. I must always keep the flame low in the stove, I thought. The meter box here at the City Building would record the amount of gas I used. If it was too much, they might ask me to pay for part of it, maybe even ask me to leave.

iv

Another job I did at the City Building was keeping the jails clean. The job actually belonged to the desk sergeant, but he subcontracted it to me for two dollars a month and I was glad to get it.

Cleaning the jails was dirty work. The men's jail was on the first floor and had four cells: a large cell called "the bull pen" and three smaller ones. The bull pen was the only cell with a commode. Older drunks considered it a matter of courtesy and seniority to be locked inside the bull pen. At times, as many as fifteen had been crowded together there. The bull pen boasted two iron cots with mattresses as rich in color as the land along the rivers. Seniority ruled here too, and the younger prisoners slept on the concrete floors.

The commode stood in the center of the room. A water pipe with a single spigot hung over the top and prisoners turned on the spigot to flush the commode. But drunks had became so bad about twisting the spigot and spraying water over fellow prisoners who took to preaching at nights that the water was now turned on outside the jail by the desk man. Whenever the commode needed flushing, a prisoner would holler, "Log in the hole!" The desk man would turn the valve. Then, "Log down!" And the water was turned off.

I was expected to clean the cells early of the mornings before school. Most times the same old faces inside the cell would grin at me and say, "Mornin', honey bucket," a term that some of the boys had brought back from the South Pacific.

Without toilets in the other three cells, the prisoners were obliged to use the floors and since they were usually pumped up on beer, they often used the walls too. The cells were heavy with the smell, and it sank into the pores of the concrete floor until no matter how hard you scrubbed it would not come out.

Another side job for me was to keep the town clock wound. This I liked. The large four-faced town clock stood on the top of the City Building. You reached it from the inside by climbing a steel spiral ladder. From this high up, you could look out over the town, the rivers, and the hills.

During the winter, from up in the tower you got the full force of the wind, and it could stiffen you out like a muskrat stretched over a board. Summers you were close enough to the sun to be scorched.

The big clock had four sides, and each side lied to time. Treasured by the Younger Women's Society, who claimed historic interest, it was permitted to lie. To be allowed to stop was a disgrace to all social citizens who moved as slowly and as uselessly as the four big hands.

The tower that housed the old clock proved to be a wonderful place for drying a hide. I hung hides on every part of the tower and clock that didn't move. What would the Younger Women's Society have said if they had known? I shuddered to think of it. But I gambled. Up so high and out in the weather, I could dry a hide in twenty-four hours and have it ready to ship.

My first winter of hanging hides inside the tower had almost proved to be a fatal one. I came from high school one day on my way to the City Building and glanced up at the clock. The hands had stopped! The wind came from the river and cut my eyes. Could I be seeing right! I rubbed my eyes and looked again, trying to gather my wits. Had anyone else in town noticed the clock? Had they climbed the spiral steps to find my hides drying peacefully there? They would run me out of the City Building! Then where would I go?

I hurried up the rungs of the spiral ladders, taking three steps at a time. A large muskrat hide had been blown by the wind into the cogs of the clock. Grabbing desperately at the hide I ripped it. Then I knew that I had done the

275

wrong thing. Small pieces of the hide remained in the moving parts of the clock. Taking out the small pieces was a slow and painful job. I was now sure that someone would come up the steps before the hide was gone. The wind was cold and my fingers so numb that I couldn't grab the slender pieces of hide. I used my teeth. It was either that or pack my clothes!

Steamboat Sam had held my job for years, and he had died while I was a small boy. But after I took on the job of clock winding, I learned of him so well that I felt I knew him. In fact, I was sometimes called Little Steamboat. He was a legend among the clock watchers of the town. He had been a town drunkard, with an art of fixing clocks. He worked on clocks better drunk than he did sober, especially the town clock. He would work out his fines for drunkenness because he couldn't pay. Whenever the town clock stopped, they'd say, "Go over to Front Street and round up Steamboat Sam. Arrest him for being drunk on the streets."

"What if he ain't drunk?"

"No need to bother with him then. If he ain't drunk he's dead."

It had been rumored that Steamboat Sam would never die. He was said to have been pickled in alcohol, preserved forever. But just the same he had died here in the valley, and the county had buried him. He got the last laugh on the taxpayers after all.

v

The women's jail was on the second floor of the City

Building. It consisted of one large room closed in by a steel door with peep holes. Inside the big room were two smaller cells with their own doors, and an old mattress lay on the concrete floor, furnishing a bed for Cardinspades Mangler. Since Cardinspades came and went as he pleased, the big steel door was seldom locked, and women brought in by the police were kept inside the smaller cells.

There were times that the big outside door was locked. Cardinspades staggered up the steps. Seeing the door to his home closed, he proceeded to bang at the steel as if he intended to cave it in. I lay in the small cot above him trying either to sleep or study. I prayed that someone on the first floor would hear his infernal pounding and come up to open the door. They usually did, and I could hear the desk man kid him. "Oh, hell!" Cardinspades would say, "you know damned well I'm too old to bother the ladies. All I want is to sleep, unless you've got enough time to get a card game going."

As a rule, there would be only one woman to worry about. Next to Cardinspades, Mountain Mouse held se-niority at the jail. She occupied the small cell nearest the outside door about three nights a week and spent the other four living with a big, dirty man named Sim Harkey in a run-down trailer over on Front Street. Her voice was shriller than a steamboat whistle and outquivered the best of the horns on the river. It was rumored that she could kill a little-boy bottle without taking it from her lips.

The first night I walked to the third floor of the City Building and heard her inside the jail, I was scared half to death. I thought she was surely dying. The big outside door was partly open and she was standing on her tiptoes looking out toward the rivers. Cardinspades was sleeping through it all, stretched out on the old mattress.

"Sim Harkey, you son of a bitch!" she screamed. "You come over here to this dump right this minute and get me out! You hear me, you son of a bitch!" And the wails that followed were enough to break down the strongest man.

She began to cry and dropped to her knees. "Oh! Help me, Lord. I know that son of a bitch is only acting like he can't hear. I'm dying."

Cardinspades rolled and tossed, raised his head, and said, "Take her, Lord. If you don't want her, pass her out so I can get some sleep. Or sober her up, and we'll play a quick game through the bars."

It was impossible to sneak past the door of the women's jail with Mountain Mouse on the inside. Her ears could have heard the droppings of a bird in the center of a two-acre field with her standing along the fence. As I crept up the stairs, she would say, "That you, Sim, honey? I knew you'd come to take me from this rat hole. I ain't used to this kind of filth, you know." And after a moment, "That's you, ain't it, Sim?"

I didn't move, hoping she would think I was gone.

"Sim! You son of a bitch! I know you're out there!"

"I'm not Sim Harkey," I would answer, praying that she'd quieten down and I could go on without listening to her scream all night.

"Well," she'd say, "good thing you ain't. I'm fixin' to kill Sim Harkey! He can find someone else to sleep with him in that trailer from now on. But don't you worry.

Me and you'll make it, honey. Pass me in a cigarette."

What time Mountain Mouse wasn't sleeping with Sim Harkey, or keeping me awake at the City Building, she was inside her favorite bootleg joint on Front Street. This particular joint was operated by a big rawboned man named Tom Butlow who allowed me inside to cleanup and run errands for customers. He spent his time eating raw stalks of horseradish and challenging his customers to target practice by lining beer cans against the walls and blowing holes in them with a Colt. And while some wino mooned over Mountain Mouse, who had dropped to her knees to mouth the beer that poured from the holes, I dodged stray bullets ricocheting off the walls and waited for Horseradish Tom to send for sand-wiches for customers. He would give me a few pennies for the errand to "hep with my ed-y-kation." The smell of the willow would be host to the wind, creep in the cracks of the joint, and sweeten somewhat the stench of women and beer.

Billy C. Clark's high school graduation picture.
Photo courtesy of Billy C. Clark.

"I never heard the two rivers hum more beautifully than they
did on the day I graduated from high school."

CHAPTER 19

I never heard the two rivers hum more beautifully than they did on the day I graduated from high school. I went to the river banks to sit and wait for commencement that night. For the first time in my life I wore a tie. One of the local policeman had tied it for me. The weather was hot. My shoes had a shine, so I walked slowly over the sand afraid that the small grains might scratch the polish. But here at the rivers I couldn't pretend. I couldn't fool them into thinking that I was someone else. I took off my shoes and wiggled my toes in the water. Small minnows that come to the rivers every May nibbled at my toes and I shook my foot and watched them scurry through the water.

High school finished. What now? College, of course! The very sound of the word scared me. It was not a new word. I had been rolling it over and over on my tongue for the past four years, since the day I entered high school, but it had never been so close! I knew where I wanted to go: the University of Kentucky. It had to be. I was a Kentuckian through and through. Would I be able to find work there? Would a man's background be unimportant? I hoped that no one else in Catlettsburg had chosen the University of Kentucky. I wanted to begin as a stranger among strangers.

That night I slipped on the cap and gown that I had rented with muskrat money. The tie stuck out like a sore thumb. I was embarrassed by it. I should have gotten someone else to tie it, I thought. What the hell did the policeman know about tying ties? He had never worn a tie himself until he joined the force.

Mom and Dad sat in the rear of the auditorium, and I knew they were watching me. I could see Mom. She had puckered her little wrinkled mouth and put her hands to her eyes. Dad reared back like he owned the world, unconcerned that he was the only man there in work clothes. Neither would have said they were proud. Our kind of people did not speak much of their emotions. You had to read it on their faces. I read it on both of theirs.

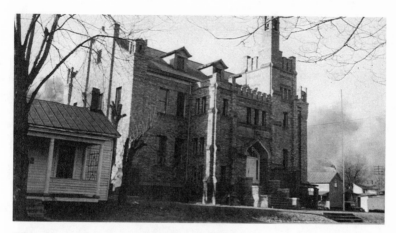

Thomas R. Brown High School, 1947.
Photo courtesy of Eleanor G. Kersey.

THE JESSE STUART FOUNDATION

The Jesse Stuart Foundation was founded in 1979 as a public, non-profit organization devoted to preserving both Jesse Stuart's literary legacy and W-Hollow, the little valley made famous in his works. The Foundation, which controls the rights to Stuart's works, is reprinting his out-of-print books and some of his never-before-published manuscripts, too.

The 730-acre Stuart farm in W-Hollow, exclusive of the home place, was turned over to the Commonwealth of Kentucky by the Stuarts in 1980. It is now designated the "Jesse Stuart Nature Preserve" and is part of the Kentucky Nature Preserves System. The Jesse Stuart Foundation is helping to develop a management plan which will ensure the preservation of W-Hollow.

The Jesse Stuart Foundation is governed by a Board of Directors consisting of University presidents, members of the Stuart family, and leaders in business, industry, and government. The Foundation also has an Executive Director, who manages its day-to-day business, plans and schedules events and meetings, coordinates publication projects, and edits a quarterly newsletter.

Associate Memberships in the Foundation are available to the general public. Associate Members will receive the newsletter, along with a Stuart book or print as a membership bonus.

For more information, contact:

The Jesse Stuart Foundation
P.O. Box 391
Ashland, KY 41114
(606)329-5232